Cambridge
Preliminary English Test
6

WITH ANSWERS

Examination papers from
University of Cambridge
ESOL Examinations

CAMBRIDGE
UNIVERSITY PRESS

CAMBRIDGE UNIVERSITY PRESS
Cambridge, New York, Melbourne, Madrid, Cape Town, Singapore,
São Paulo, Delhi, Dubai, Tokyo

Cambridge University Press
The Edinburgh Building, Cambridge CB2 8RU, UK

www.cambridge.org
Information on this title: www.cambridge.org/9780521123198

First published 2010
Reprinted 2010

Printed in the United Kingdom at the University Press, Cambridge

A catalogue record for this publication is available from the British Library

ISBN 978-0-521-123198 Student's Book with answers
ISBN 978-0-521-123167 Student's Book without answers
ISBN 978-0-521-123211 Audio CD Set
ISBN 978-0-521-123242 Self-study Pack

Cambridge University Press has no responsibility for the persistence or
accuracy of URLs for external or third-party internet websites referred to in
this publication, and does not guarantee that any content on such websites is,
or will remain, accurate or appropriate. Information regarding prices, travel
timetables and other factual information given in this work are correct at
the time of first printing but Cambridge University Press does not guarantee
the accuracy of such information thereafter.

Contents

A Guide to PET

The PET examination is part of a group of examinations developed by Cambridge ESOL called the Cambridge Main Suite. The Main Suite consists of five examinations which have similar characteristics but are designed for different levels of English language ability. Within the five levels, PET is at Level B1 (Threshold) in the *Council of Europe's Common European Framework of Reference for Languages: Learning, teaching, assessment.* It has also been accredited in the UK as an Entry Level 3 ESOL certificate in the National Qualifications Framework.

Examination	Council of Europe Framework Level	UK National Qualifications Framework Level
CPE Certificate of Proficiency in English	C2	3
CAE Certificate in Advanced English	C1	2
FCE First Certificate in English	B2	1
PET Preliminary English Test	B1	Entry 3
KET Key English Test	A2	Entry 2

PET is a popular exam with candidates who are learning English out of personal interest and for those who are studying for employment reasons. It is also useful preparation for higher level exams, such as FCE (First Certificate in English), CAE (Certificate in Advanced English) and CPE (Certificate of Proficiency in English).

If you can deal with everyday written and spoken communications (e.g. read simple textbooks and articles, write simple personal letters, make notes during a meeting), then this is the exam for you.

Topics

These are the topics used in the PET exam:

Clothes
Daily life
Education
Entertainment and media
Environment
Food and drink
Free time
Health, medicine and
  exercise

Hobbies and leisure
House and home
Language
Natural world
People
Personal feelings, opinions
  and experiences
Personal identification
Places and buildings

Relations with other people
Services
Shopping
Social interaction
Sport
Transport
Travel and holidays
Weather
Work and jobs

PET content: an overview

Paper	Name	Timing	Content	Test focus
Paper 1	Reading/ Writing	1 hour 30 minutes	Reading: Five parts which test a range of reading skills with a variety of texts, ranging from very short notices to longer continuous texts. Writing: Three parts which test a range of writing skills.	Assessment of candidates' ability to understand the meaning of written English at word, phrase, sentence, paragraph and whole text level. Assessment of candidates' ability to produce straightforward written English, ranging from producing variations on simple sentences to pieces of continuous text.
Paper 2	Listening	35 minutes (approx.)	Four parts ranging from short exchanges to longer dialogues and monologues.	Assessment of candidates' ability to understand dialogues and monologues in both informal and neutral settings on a range of everyday topics.
Paper 3	Speaking	10–12 minutes per pair of candidates	Four parts: In Part 1, candidates interact with an examiner; In Parts 2 and 4, they interact with another candidate; In Part 3, they have an extended individual long turn.	Assessment of candidates' ability to express themselves in order to carry out functions at *Threshold* level. To ask and to understand questions and make appropriate responses. To talk freely on matters of personal interest.

Paper 1: Reading and Writing

Paper format
The Reading component contains five parts. The Writing component contains three parts.

Number of questions
Reading has 35 questions; Writing has seven questions.

Sources
Authentic and adapted-authentic real world notices; newspapers and magazines; simplified encyclopaedias; brochures and leaflets; websites.

Answering
Candidates indicate answers by shading lozenges (Reading), or writing answers (Writing) on an answer sheet.

Timing
1 hour 30 minutes.

Marks
Reading: Each of the 35 questions carries one mark. This is weighted so that this comprises 25% of total marks for the whole examination.

Writing: Questions 1–5 carry one mark each. Question 6 is marked out of five; and Question 7/8 is marked out of 15. This gives a total of 25 which represents 25% of total marks for the whole examination.

Preparing for the Reading component

To prepare for the Reading component, you should read a variety of authentic texts, for example, newspapers and magazines, non-fiction books, and other sources of factual material, such as leaflets, brochures and websites. It is also a good idea to practise reading (and writing) short communicative messages, including notes, cards and emails. Remember you won't always need to understand every word in order to be able to do a task in the exam.

Before the examination, think about the time you need to do each part. It is usually approximately 50 minutes on the Reading component and 40 minutes on the Writing component.

Reading			
Part	Task Type and Format	Task Focus	Number of Questions
1	Three-option multiple choice. Five short discrete texts: signs and messages, postcards, notes, emails, labels, etc., plus one example.	Reading real-world notices and other short texts for the main message.	5
2	Matching. Five items in the form of descriptions of people to match to eight short adapted-authentic texts.	Reading multiple texts for specific information and detailed comprehension.	5
3	True/False. Ten items with an adapted-authentic long text.	Processing a factual text. Scanning for specific information while disregarding redundant material.	10
4	Four-option multiple choice. Five items with an adapted-authentic long text.	Reading for detailed comprehension: understanding attitude, opinion and writer purpose. Reading for gist, inference and global meaning.	5
5	Four-option multiple-choice cloze. Ten items, plus an integrated example, with an adapted-authentic text drawn from a variety of sources. The text is of a factual or narrative nature.	Understanding of vocabulary and grammar in a short text, and understanding the lexico-structural patterns in the text.	10

Preparing for the Writing component

Part 1

You have to complete five sentences which will test your grammar. There is an example, showing exactly what the task involves. You should write between one and three words to fill this gap. The second sentence, when complete, must mean the same as the first sentence.

It is essential to spell correctly and no marks will be given if a word is misspelled. You will also lose the mark if you produce an answer of more than three words, even if your writing includes the correct answer.

Part 2

You have to produce a short communicative message of between 35 and 45 words in length. You are told who you are writing to and why, and you must include three content points. These are clearly laid out with bullet points in the question. To gain top marks, all three points must be in your answer, so it is important to read the question carefully and plan what you will include. Marks will not be deducted for minor errors.

Before the exam, you need to practise writing answers of the correct length. Answers that are too short or too long will probably lose marks.

The General Mark Scheme below is used with a Task-specific Mark Scheme (see pages 104, 117, 129 and 141).

General Mark Scheme for Writing Part 2

Mark	Criteria
5	All content elements covered appropriately. Message clearly communicated to reader.
4	All content elements adequately dealt with. Message communicated successfully, on the whole.
3	All content elements attempted. Message requires some effort by the reader. or One content element omitted but others clearly communicated.
2	Two content elements omitted, or unsuccessfully dealt with. Message only partly communicated to reader. or Script may be slightly short (20–25 words).
1	Little relevant content and/or message requires excessive effort by the reader, or short (10–19 words).
0	Totally irrelevant or totally incomprehensible or too short (under 10 words).

Part 3

You have a choice of task: either a story or an informal letter. You need to write about 100 words. Answers below 80 words will receive fewer marks. Answers longer than 100 words may receive fewer marks.

Make sure you practise enough before the exam. Reading simplified readers in English will give you ideas for story writing. Also writing to a penfriend or e-pal will give you useful practice.

Mark Scheme for Writing Part 3

Band 5 – the candidate's writing fully achieves the desired effect on the target reader. The use of language will be confident and ambitious for the level, including a wide range of structures and vocabulary within the task set. Coherence, within the constraints of the level, will be achieved by the use of simple linking devices, and the response will be well organised. Errors which do occur will be minor and non-impeding, perhaps due to ambitious attempts at more complex language. Overall, no effort will be required of the reader.

Band 4 – the candidate's writing will achieve the desired effect on the target reader. The use of language will be fairly ambitious for the level, including a range of structures and vocabulary within the task set. There will be some linking of sentences and evidence of organisation. Some errors will occur, although these will be generally non-impeding. Overall, only a little effort will be required of the reader.

Band 3 – the candidate's writing may struggle at times to achieve the desired effect on the target reader. The use of language, including the range of structure and vocabulary, will be unambitious, or, if ambitious, it will be flawed. There will be some attempt at organisation but the linking of sentences will not always be maintained. A number of errors may be present, although these will be mostly non-impeding. Overall, some effort will be required of the reader.

Band 2 – the candidate's writing struggles to achieve the desired effect on the target reader. The use of language, including the range of structure and vocabulary, will tend to be simplistic, limited, or repetitive. The response may be incoherent, and include erratic use of punctuation. There will be numerous errors which will sometimes impede communication. Overall, considerable effort will be required of the reader.

Band 1 – the candidate's writing has a negative effect on the target reader. The use of language will be severely restricted, and there will be no evidence of a range of structures and vocabulary. The response will be seriously incoherent, and may include an absence of punctuation. Language will be very poorly controlled and the response will be difficult to understand. Overall, excessive effort will be required of the reader.

Band 0 – there may be too little language for assessment, or the response may be totally illegible; the content may be impossible to understand, or completely irrelevant to the task.

Writing			
Part	Task Type and Format	Task Focus	Number of Questions
1	Sentence transformations. Five items, plus an integrated example, that are theme-related. Candidates are given sentences and then asked to complete similar sentences using a different structural pattern so that the sentence still has the same meaning.	Control and understanding of Threshold/PET grammatical structures. Rephrasing and reformulating information.	5
2	Short communicative message. Candidates are prompted to write a short message in the form of a postcard, note, email, etc. The prompt takes the form of a rubric to respond to.	A short piece of writing of 35–45 words focusing on communication of specific messages.	1
3	A longer piece of continuous writing. There is a choice of two questions, an informal letter or a story. Candidates are primarily assessed on their ability to use and control a range of Threshold-level language. Coherent organisation, spelling and punctuation are also assessed.	Writing about 100 words focusing on control and range of language.	1

Paper 2: Listening

Paper format
This paper contains four parts.

Number of questions
25

Text types
All texts are based on authentic situations.

Answering
Candidates indicate answers either by shading lozenges (Parts 1, 2 and 4) or writing answers (Part 3) on an answer sheet. Candidates record their answers on the question paper as they listen. They are then given six minutes at the end of the test to copy these on to the answer sheet.

Recording information
Each text is heard twice. Recordings will contain a variety of accents corresponding to standard variants of native speaker accents.

Timing
About 35 minutes, including six minutes to transfer answers.

Marks
Each question carries one mark. This gives a total of 25 marks, which represents 25% of total marks for the whole examination.

Part	Task Type and Format	Task Focus	Number of questions
1	Multiple choice (discrete). Short neutral or informal monologues or dialogues. Seven discrete three-option multiple-choice items with visuals, plus one example.	Listening to identify key information from short exchanges.	7
2	Multiple choice. Longer monologue or interview (with one main speaker). Six three-option multiple-choice items.	Listening to identify specific information and detailed meaning.	6
3	Gap-fill. Longer monologue. Six gaps to fill in. Candidates need to write one or more words in each space.	Listening to identify, understand and interpret information.	6
4	True/False. Longer informal dialogue. Candidates need to decide whether six statements are correct or incorrect.	Listening for detailed meaning, and to identify the attitudes and opinions of the speakers.	6

Preparing for the Listening paper

You will hear the instructions for each task on the recording, and see them on the exam paper.
In Part 1, there is also an example text and task to show you how to record your answers.
In Parts 2, 3 and 4, the instructions are followed by a pause; you should read the questions in that part then. This will help you prepare for the listening.

The best preparation for the listening paper is to listen to authentic spoken English at this level. Having discussions provides a good authentic source of listening practice, as does listening to the teacher. You can also listen to texts to give you practice in understanding different voices and styles of delivery.

Paper 3: Speaking

Paper format
The standard format is two candidates and two examiners. One of the examiners acts as an interlocutor and the other as an assessor. The interlocutor directs the test, while the assessor takes no part in the interaction.

Timing
10–12 minutes per pair of candidates.

Marks
Candidates are assessed on their performance throughout the test. There are a total of 25 marks in Paper 3, making 25% of the total score for the whole examination.

Part	Task Type and Format	Task Focus	Timing
1	Each candidate interacts with the interlocutor. The interlocutor asks the candidates questions in turn, using standardised questions.	Giving information of a factual, personal kind. The candidates respond to questions about present circumstances, past experiences and future plans.	2–3 minutes
2	Simulated situation. Candidates interact with each other. Visual stimulus is given to the candidates to aid the discussion task. The interlocutor sets up the activity using a standardised rubric.	Using functional language to make and respond to suggestions, discuss alternatives, make recommendations and negotiate agreement.	2–3 minutes
3	Extended turn. A colour photograph is given to each candidate in turn and they are asked to talk about it for up to a minute. Both photographs relate to the same topic.	Describing photographs and managing discourse, using appropriate vocabulary, in a longer turn.	3 minutes
4	General conversation. Candidates interact with each other. The topic of the conversation develops the theme established in Part 3. The interlocutor sets up the activity using a standardised rubric.	The candidates talk together about their opinions, likes/dislikes, preferences, experiences, habits, etc.	3 minutes

Assessment

Throughout the test, you are assessed on your language skills, not your personality, intelligence or knowledge of the world. You must, however, be prepared to develop the conversation, where appropriate, and respond to the tasks set. Prepared speeches are not acceptable.

You are assessed on your own individual performance and not in relation to each other. Both examiners assess you. The interlocutor awards a mark for global achievement; the assessor awards marks for: Grammar and Vocabulary, Discourse Management, Pronunciation and Interactive Communication.

Grammar and Vocabulary
This refers to the accurate use of grammatical forms and appropriate use of vocabulary. It also includes the range of vocabulary. Performance is viewed in terms of the overall effectiveness of the language used in dealing with the tasks.

Discourse Management
This refers to the coherence, extent and relevance of each individual's contribution. On this scale, the ability to maintain a coherent flow of language is assessed, either within a single utterance or over a string of utterances. Also assessed here is how relevant the contributions are to what has gone before.

Pronunciation
This refers to the candidate's ability to produce comprehensible utterances to fulfil the task requirements. This includes stress, intonation, and individual sounds. Examiners put themselves in the position of the non-language specialist and assess the overall impact of the pronunciation and the degree of effort required to understand the candidate. Different varieties of English, e.g. British, North American, Australian, etc., are acceptable, provided they are used consistently throughout the test.

Interactive Communication
This scale refers to the candidate's ability to use language to achieve meaningful communication. This includes initiating and responding without undue hesitation, the ability to use interactive strategies to maintain or repair communication, and sensitivity to the norms of turn-taking.

Further information

More information about PET or any other Cambridge ESOL examination can be obtained from Cambridge ESOL at the address below or from the website at www.CambridgeESOL.org

University of Cambridge ESOL Examinations
1 Hills Road
Cambridge CB1 2EU
United Kingdom

Telephone +44 1223 553355
Fax: +44 1223 460278
email: ESOLHelpdesk@Cambridgeassessment.org.uk

Test 1

PAPER 1   READING AND WRITING TEST   (1 hour 30 minutes)

READING

Part 1

Questions 1–5

Look at the text in each question.
What does it say?
Mark the correct letter **A**, **B** or **C** on your answer sheet.

Example:

0

A Buy three films for the price of two.

B Get a free film with every one you buy.

C Films bought here are printed free.

Answer:

1

Who should Lisa contact if she wants to go to the concert?

A Yvonne

B Marie

C Sally

12

2

Parking Form

Complete and place in lower left-hand corner of windscreen

Car registration ....

Date ....

A Register your car here by filling in this form.

B Put this form in your car windscreen after filling it in.

C Place the completed form at the top of your car windscreen.

3

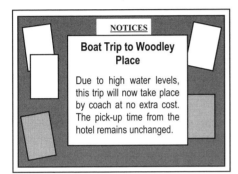

NOTICES

Boat Trip to Woodley Place

Due to high water levels, this trip will now take place by coach at no extra cost. The pick-up time from the hotel remains unchanged.

What has changed about the trip to Woodley Place?

A the transport

B the price

C the departure time

4

Mum,
Could you pick up my skirt from the dry cleaner's when you collect your jacket? I'll pay you back this evening.
Thanks.
                        Sonja

What will Sonja's mother do?

A receive money for the dry cleaning from Sonja tonight

B fetch Sonja's jacket from the dry cleaner's for her

C deliver her own clothes to the dry cleaner's

5

Allow at least two hours for your visit to the castle

A Each tour of the castle lasts less than two hours.

B Two hours is the minimum time recommended for a visit to the castle.

C Visitors are only allowed to spend two hours inside the castle.

Part 2

Questions 6–10

The people below live in London and are all interested in keeping fit.
On the opposite page there are descriptions of eight websites for people wanting to keep fit.
Decide which website would be the most suitable for the following people.
For questions **6–10**, mark the correct letter (**A–H**) on your answer sheet.

---

6  Klara has recently moved to London and enjoys serious running. She is looking for a club where she can take part in competitions.

7  Sami wants to find some ideas for keeping fit at home and communicate online with other people doing the same thing. He doesn't want to have to pay for using the website.

8  Kumiko is a member of a local gym where she goes at least twice a week. She does not get much time to shop, so wants to buy gym clothes and shoes online.

9  Peter loves the outdoors and cycles to different places each weekend to keep fit. He wants a website which will give him suggestions for a range of suitable destinations.

10  Stefano is a student and is looking for a gym where he can keep fit. He wants to pay each time he visits the gym rather than paying a fee to become a member.

FIND THE PERFECT WAY TO KEEP FIT WITH THESE WEBSITES

A **www.activelife.co.uk** This site is perfect for those who like to combine living a healthy lifestyle with enjoying the countryside. Type in the name of the town and you get a list of locations that offer routes for cycling or exploring the area on foot. There is also information on cycling competitions in Britain.

B **www.fitinfo.com** This online shop offers books, magazines, DVDs and software connected to keeping fit. You simply type in the aspect of keeping fit that you are interested in, such as 'keeping fit outdoors', and a super selection is displayed.

C **www.fitnet.co.uk** Steve Amos started this site for busy people wanting to keep fit. Fill in a questionnaire and Steve will create a fitness programme for you. Although Steve's fee is high, you can email him for advice whenever you want. In addition, Steve has designed a range of fitness clothes and footwear, which anyone can order (48-hour delivery).

D **www.NAG.co.uk** The National Athletics Group is a site for people interested in athletics. It allows you to find out where your nearest athletics club is and provides information about races and other athletics events around the country. There is a popular chatroom where athletes exchange suggestions and ideas.

E **www.swavedon.com** Swavedon is a national park with a lake, which offers many different ways of keeping fit in the great outdoors. There are three cycle routes, a jogging track around the lake and several woodland walks.

F **www.fitnessonline.co.uk** This is a free government website that encourages people to keep fit. It gives diet advice, and allows you to work through a fitness programme without leaving your house. It also offers advice on gym equipment to buy and has a chatroom, where you can compare experiences with others.

G **www.fitnessclub.co.uk** This website tells you all you need to know about this chain of gyms, including where your nearest Fitnessclub gym is, how you can become a member and how much the yearly fee is. Advice is given on everything from using a running machine to buying the right equipment. Each gym has a swimming pool and a shop selling gymwear.

H **www.sportsarena.co.uk** This website tells you how you can keep fit at this group of London sports centres. You don't have to be a member – these centres operate a pay-as-you-go system. They all have a pool, squash courts, gym and outdoor tennis courts. The website includes details of locations, opening times and prices.

Part 3

Questions 11–20

Look at the sentences below about a book club.
Read the text on the opposite page to decide if each sentence is correct or incorrect.
If it is correct, mark **A** on your answer sheet.
If it is not correct, mark **B** on your answer sheet.

11   By ordering a book, you qualify to become a member of the International Book Club.

12   Every new member can request a watch from the book club.

13   You can buy a DVD more cheaply when you join.

14   All club books cost half the publisher's price.

15   Each club magazine gives you a choice of over 1,000 books.

16   You get a different choice of books if you order from the website.

17   One special book is recommended every month.

18   You may receive a book that the club has chosen for you.

19   You must pay the postage when sending your application to join the club.

20   You should pay as soon as you receive your books.

International Book Club

Have you ever thought of joining a book club and buying new books through the post? Here at the International Book Club, we already have many members buying books from us by mail.

To join:
You just need to send us your first order from our book list.

Immediate benefits:

- As a special offer, you may choose any reduced-price books from our new members' book list, to the value of £6 in total (plus postage and packing). By doing this, you will save pounds on the publishers' prices.
- Tick the box on your form to order a free watch.
- If you reply within seven days, we will send you another free gift carefully chosen from our book list by our staff.
- Order a DVD from the many on offer in our list, at half the recommended retail price.

When you've joined:
As a member, you'll enjoy savings of between 30% and 50% off the publisher's price on every book you buy, and what's more, they'll come straight to your door. Your free club magazine arrives once a month, to keep you up to date with the latest best-sellers. This means that every year we offer over 1,000 books to choose from. On the Internet, you can find all our titles for the year on our exclusive members' website.

Being a member:
All we are asking you to do while you are a member is to choose four books during your first year. After that, you can decide on the number of books you wish to take.

In each of our monthly club magazines, our experienced staff choose a Club Choice book – a work of fiction or a reference title which they feel is particularly worth buying, and which is offered at an extra-special price. However, if you do not want this book, just say so in the space provided on the form. We will always send the book if we do not receive this.

So, return your application form today, but hurry – it's not every day we can make you an offer like this. To apply to become a member, all you need to do is simply fill in the enclosed form and return it in the postage-paid envelope supplied.

Before you know it, your books will be with you. Please don't send any money now, as we will send you your bill with the books. And remember, you have up to a fortnight to decide if you wish to keep the books you have ordered. You should then either return the books or send your payment.

Part 4

Questions 21–25

Read the text and questions below.
For each question, mark the correct letter **A**, **B**, **C** or **D** on your answer sheet.

Rock Band

Two years ago, our 14-year-old son, Ben, asked us for a set of drums for his birthday. At first, we were very much against the idea because of the noise. 'It's better than watching television or playing computer games in my free time,' Ben argued, 'and it'll keep me out of trouble.' In the end we gave in. 'All right,' we said, 'but you must consider the rest of the family and the neighbours when you play.'

That was just the beginning. Because drums are not the easiest instruments to transport, the other members of Ben's band started appearing at our home with their guitars and other electrical equipment. And so, for several hours a week, the house shakes to the noise of their instruments and their teenage singing.

At least Ben's hobby has been good for our health: whenever the band start practising, my husband and I go out for a long walk. And I must admit that, although their music may sound a little strange, they are a friendly and polite group of young men. I cannot judge their musical skill – after all I didn't expect my parents' generation to like the same music as I did when I was a teenager – but they do play regularly in local clubs for young people.

Our main worry is that they won't spend enough time on their school work because of their musical activities, though this hasn't happened yet. I am always stressing to Ben how important his studies are. But one thing is certain – Ben was right: it has kept him out of trouble and he is never bored.

21 What is the writer trying to do in this text?

    A   complain about her son's friends
    B   give advice to teenagers
    C   describe her son's hobby
    D   compare herself with her parents

22 Why did the writer give Ben the present he wanted?

    A   She wanted to reward him for working hard.
    B   He already had too many computer games.
    C   She knew he would use it sensibly.
    D   He persuaded her it would be a good idea.

23 Why do the band always practise at Ben's house?

- **A** It is difficult for Ben to move his drums.
- **B** The neighbours don't mind the noise.
- **C** Ben's parents enjoy listening to them.
- **D** They can leave their equipment there.

24 What does the writer say about the band members?

- **A** Their influence on her son worries her.
- **B** Their taste in music is different from hers.
- **C** They play their instruments well.
- **D** They avoid any contact with her.

25 What might the writer say to her son?

A Your teacher has just phoned. He wants to know why you weren't at school today.

B When are you playing at the club next? Dad and I would love to come along again.

C If you don't know what to do with yourself, there's a good programme on the television in a few minutes.

D Are you sure you've finished your homework? It's more important than band practice.

Part 5

Questions 26–35

Read the text below and choose the correct word for each space.
For each question, mark the correct letter **A**, **B**, **C** or **D** on your answer sheet.

Example:

0	**A** most	**B** more	**C** best	**D** better

Answer:

0	A B C D
	▬ ▭ ▭ ▭

Tom Cruise

Tom Cruise is one of the **(0)** .... successful actors in cinema history. However, life hasn't always been that easy for him. As a young boy, Tom was shy and had **(26)** .... in finding friends, although he really enjoyed **(27)** .... part in school plays.

(28) .... he had finished High School, Tom went to New York to look for work. He found employment as a porter, and at the same time he **(29)** .... drama classes. In 1980, the film director Franco Zeffirelli **(30)** .... Tom his first part in a film. Ten years later, he had become **(31)** .... successful that he was one of the highest-paid actors in Hollywood, **(32)** .... millions of dollars for **(33)** .... film.

Today, Tom **(34)** .... appears in films and is as **(35)** .... as ever with his thousands of fans from all around the world.

26	**A** worry	**B** problem	**C** fear	**D** difficulty
27	**A** making	**B** holding	**C** taking	**D** finding
28	**A** While	**B** During	**C** After	**D** Until
29	**A** prepared	**B** waited	**C** attended	**D** happened
30	**A** suggested	**B** offered	**C** tried	**D** advised
31	**A** so	**B** such	**C** too	**D** very
32	**A** paying	**B** earning	**C** winning	**D** reaching
33	**A** another	**B** all	**C** each	**D** some
34	**A** yet	**B** ever	**C** already	**D** still
35	**A** popular	**B** favourite	**C** preferred	**D** approved

WRITING

Part 1

Questions 1–5

Here are some sentences about learning Italian.
For each question, complete the second sentence so that it means the same as the first.
Use no more than three words.
Write only the missing words on your answer sheet.
You may use this page for any rough work.

Example:

0   Daniel started Italian classes six months ago.

     Daniel's had Italian classes .... **six months**.

Answer: | **0** | *for* |

---

1   After seeing an advertisement for Italian lessons, Daniel decided to go.

     Daniel .... **an advertisement for Italian lessons and then decided to go**.

2   There are fifteen other students in his Italian class.

     His Italian class .... **fifteen other students in it**.

3   Daniel thinks that speaking Italian is easier than writing it.

     Daniel doesn't think that speaking is .... **as writing Italian**.

4   Daniel's teacher is Italian and her name's Chiara Paolozzi.

     Daniel's teacher is Italian and she's .... **Chiara Paolozzi**.

5   The students are given two hours of homework each week.

     Each week Chiara .... **the students two hours of homework**.

Part 2

Question 6

You have spent the weekend staying with some English friends.

Write a card to them. In your card, you should

- thank your friends for the weekend
- say what you enjoyed most about the weekend
- invite them to stay with you.

Write **35–45 words** on your answer sheet.

Part 3

Write an answer to **one** of the questions (**7** or **8**) in this part.
Write your answer in about **100 words** on your answer sheet.
Mark the question number in the box at the top of your answer sheet.

Question 7

- This is part of a letter you receive from an English friend.

> I've just seen a brilliant programme about dolphins on television. Which programmes have you enjoyed recently? How much television do you watch?

- Now write a letter, answering your penfriend's questions.
- Write your **letter** on your answer sheet.

Question 8

- Your English teacher has asked you to write a story.
- This is the title for your story:

Walking in the rain

- Write your **story** on your answer sheet.

PAPER 2   LISTENING TEST   approx 35 minutes
(including 6 minutes transfer time)

Part 1

Questions 1–7

There are seven questions in this part.
For each question there are three pictures and a short recording.
Choose the correct picture and put a tick (✓) in the box below it.

Example: Where is the girl's hat?

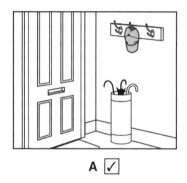 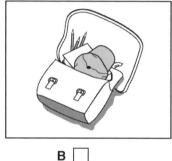 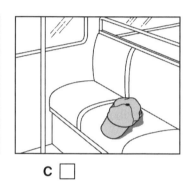

A ✓   B ☐   C ☐

---

1   Where will the friends meet?

A ☐   B ☐   C ☐

2   What has the girl forgotten to bring?

A ☐   B ☐   C ☐

3 Which TV programme is on at 9 o'clock tonight?

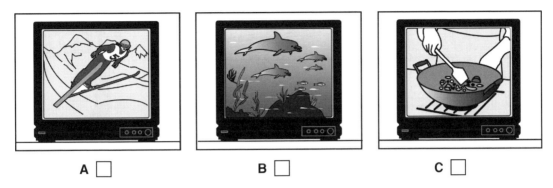

A ☐   B ☐   C ☐

4 How will the man book tickets for the show?

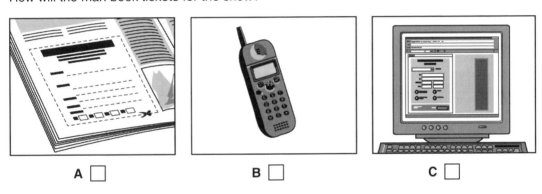

A ☐   B ☐   C ☐

5 What will the man do this winter?

A ☐   B ☐   C ☐

6   How does the man want the woman to help him?

A ☐   B ☐   C ☐

7   Which house did the woman stay in?

A ☐   B ☐   C ☐

Part 2

Questions 8–13

You will hear a news reporter called Angela Bond, talking on the radio about her job.
For each question, put a tick (✓) in the correct box.

---

8 Where is Angela working at the moment?

    A ☐ Britain

    B ☐ the USA

    C ☐ Asia

9 Angela likes her job because she

    A ☐ loves being in dangerous situations.

    B ☐ never knows where she'll go next.

    C ☐ enjoys watching important events happen.

10 What did Angela bring home from Hong Kong?

    A ☐ pictures

    B ☐ carpets

    C ☐ furniture

11 What time does Angela's working day begin?

    A ☐ 8.30 am

    B ☐ 6.30 pm

    C ☐ 10.00 am

12 Where did Angela meet her boyfriend?

A ☐ at her sister's house

B ☐ at university

C ☐ in Hong Kong

13 What does Angela do to relax?

A ☐ She cooks a meal.

B ☐ She goes sailing.

C ☐ She goes shopping.

Part 3

Questions 14–19

You will hear a radio programme about some historic places to visit.
For each question, fill in the missing information in the numbered space.

HISTORIC PLACES TO VISIT

Black Rock Caves

- Over 2 million years old
- For half a million years, people and animals, especially **(14)** .... , lived here
- Special evening tours during the month of **(15)** ....

Salter House

- Built in the year **(16)** ....
- Made famous by the television series called *Aunt Dorothy*
- All visitors want to see Dorothy's **(17)** ....

The Old Port

- Have a ride on an old tram to the **(18)** .... village
- In the factory, find out how people used to make **(19)** ....

Part 4

Questions 20–25

Look at the six sentences for this part.
You will hear a conversation between a boy, Marcus, and a girl, Catherine, about their homework.
Decide if each sentence is correct or incorrect.
If it is correct, put a tick (✓) in the box under **A** for **YES**. If it is not correct, put a tick (✓) in the box under **B** for **NO**.

		A YES	B NO
20	Catherine finds it hard to understand why Marcus has so much homework.	☐	☐
21	Marcus agrees that he could change his weekend activities.	☐	☐
22	Catherine thinks visiting the museum was a good experience for Marcus.	☐	☐
23	Catherine offers to show Marcus the maths homework she has already done.	☐	☐
24	Marcus worries that his teacher might be angry if Catherine helps him.	☐	☐
25	After talking to Catherine, Marcus feels more confident about his homework.	☐	☐

About the Speaking test

The Speaking test lasts about 10 to 12 minutes. You take the test with another candidate. There are two examiners in the room. One examiner talks to you and the other examiner listens to you. Both the examiners give you marks.

Part 1

The examiners introduce themselves and then one examiner asks you and your partner to say your names and spell them. This examiner then asks you questions about yourself, your daily life, interests, etc.

Part 2

The examiner asks you to talk about something together and gives you a drawing to help you.

Part 3

You each have a chance to talk by yourselves. The examiner gives you a colour photograph to look at and asks you to talk about it. When you have finished talking, the examiner gives your partner a different photograph to look at and to talk about.

Part 4

The examiner asks you and your partner to say more about the subject of the photographs in Part 3. You may be asked to give your opinion or to talk about something that has happened to you.

Test 2

PAPER 1   READING AND WRITING TEST   (1 hour 30 minutes)

READING

Part 1

Questions 1–5

Look at the text in each question.
What does it say?
Mark the correct letter **A**, **B** or **C** on your answer sheet.

Example:

0

A Do not leave your bicycle touching the window.

B Broken glass may damage your bicycle tyres.

C Your bicycle may not be safe here.

Answer:

1

WATCH REPAIRS

Warning to Customers

All uncollected items will be sold after twelve months.

A This shop will sell customers' watches within twelve months.

B This shop will keep customers' watches for up to twelve months.

C This shop will look after customers' watches for more than twelve months.

2

Philippe,

Couldn't wait any longer, didn't want to miss the start of the match! Problem at work? Here's your ticket – see you at the stadium.

Stefano

A Philippe and Stefano missed each other at the stadium.

B Stefano had to leave without Philippe to get to work.

C Stefano has given up waiting for Philippe to arrive.

3

PARENTS:

Complete and return your child's form for next month's school trip by Friday

A Parents must return forms this week if their child is going on Friday's trip.

B Parents cannot go on next month's trip unless they return their forms by Friday.

C The last day for returning completed forms for the trip is Friday.

4

From:	Gabi
To:	Jo

I'll be in town on business on Wednesday, so could we meet for dinner then, instead of on Thursday as usual?

Gabi wants Jo to

A change an arrangement.

B cancel a regular event.

C come to a business meeting.

5

A It is not possible to use the lift above the ground floor today.

B The lift will not be going to the basement today.

C The stairs between the basement and the ground floor are closed today.

Part 2

Questions 6–10

The people below all want to visit a park.
On the opposite page there are descriptions of eight parks.
Decide which park would be the most suitable for the following people.
For questions **6–10**, mark the correct letter (**A–H**) on your answer sheet.

6  Isabel works in the city centre and likes painting and drawing in her free time. She wants to practise her hobby in a small, quiet park near her office.

7  Mr Martin wants to take his eight-year-old pupils to a park anywhere within the city, with lots of organised activities which allow the children to read about local wildlife they may see.

8  Kumiko and Atsuko would like to visit a park which they can get to by boat. They want to buy lunch there and then enjoy a short walk accompanied by an expert leader.

9  Hans and Birgit Kaufmann and their family want to visit a park which is historically important. Their teenage children would like to try a water sport.

10  Melanie and Stefan are students who need to visit a busy park for a college project. They want to draw people taking part in team sports and watching entertainment.

PARKS IN AND AROUND THE CITY

A Hadley Park

This park is in the peaceful village of Cranford, 20 km outside the city. The park has large green spaces for football and there is also an area of woodland, a boating lake, fish ponds and a variety of local wildlife. The public car park is free.

B Highdown Park

The largest and most popular open space in the city, Highdown has many paths for keen walkers, as well as horse-riding and golf. The much-visited 19th-century glasshouses contain an interesting exhibition about birds from around the world.

C Brock Park

A beautiful park on the edge of the city, Brock Park attracts huge crowds. The open-air theatre has a programme of plays suitable for school groups. There is a well-used basketball court and baseball field, a children's playground and a café. Climb Harry's Hill to admire the beautiful fields and forests beyond the city.

D Lilac Park and House

This busy city-centre park has a long history dating back to the 1700s, when it belonged to the writer Thomas Crane. The house is open to the public and a guided visit can also include a walk around the famous rose gardens, finishing at the popular Butterfly Café.

E Boscawen Park

This small and peaceful park offers guided tours, given by the knowledgeable Environment Officers, and evening visitors to the park may be lucky enough to see rare frogs and bats. It is situated on the River Elton and can be reached in about 30 minutes from the city centre by river taxi. There is a snack bar and gift shop.

F East Bank Park

This is a tiny, little-known park in the heart of the city, with gardens filled with sculptures, trees and flowers. It makes a perfect resting place, popular with local artists, and is within minutes of the theatre and entertainment district.

G Victoria Park

This quiet park, on the edge of the city and easy to visit by public transport, has boats for hire on the lake, a skateboard park, basketball and tennis courts and a picnic area. Often seen in postcard views of the city, Victoria Park contains one of the oldest windmills in the country – the museum should not be missed.

H Elmwood Park

At Elmwood Park, there are walks on well-made paths and cycle rides for all abilities. Elmwood is just inside the city limit and has an area of quiet woodland, which is home to deer and other animals. The visitor centre, numerous display boards and a fun quiz make this a positive learning experience for all ages.

Part 3

Questions 11–20

Look at the sentences below about the Iditarod Trail in Alaska.
Read the text on the opposite page to decide if each sentence is correct or incorrect.
If it is correct, mark **A** on your answer sheet.
If it is not correct, mark **B** on your answer sheet.

11 The population of Alaska remained the same throughout the 1880s.

12 For a short time, more people lived in Iditarod than in any other city in Alaska.

13 After 1910, it became possible to deliver letters in winter as well as summer.

14 When travelling on the Iditarod Trail, drivers had to take food for the dogs with them.

15 In the 1920s, aeroplanes were used more often than boats and dogs.

16 Doctors in Nome had a good supply of medicine to cure diphtheria.

17 The pilot Carl Eielson refused to fly his plane because of the cold weather.

18 Leonhard Seppala's dog was able to lead him safely to his destination.

19 Balto fell into some icy water but managed to save himself.

20 The Iditarod race takes a different route every year.

THE HISTORY OF THE IDITAROD – THE LAST GREAT RACE ON EARTH

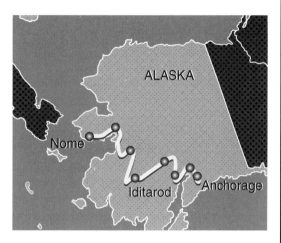

In the 1880s, gold was discovered in what is now the most northern state of the USA, Alaska. Many people came to the area hoping to get rich. New towns were built and grew quickly. One such town was called Iditarod, which means 'far, distant place'. This town grew so quickly during 1909 that it briefly became the largest city in Alaska. In the summer months, essential supplies could be delivered to these towns by boat, but in the winter the rivers and the ocean froze and there was no way to get to them. So, in 1910, a winter track was built which would be used by teams of dogs pulling sleds. They would take mail, food and clothes to the gold miners.

The track became known as the Iditarod Trail. It took a team of dogs about three weeks to travel across Alaska. They stopped at 'roadhouses' where the drivers could get a warm bed for the night and something to eat for both themselves and their dogs. The trail was used every winter until the 1920s when aeroplanes replaced steam boats and dog teams as the main form of transport.

However, the dogs had one last taste of fame in 1925, when a disease called diphtheria hit the city of Nome. The disease could be cured, but, unfortunately, the closest medicine that could be found was in Anchorage, right on the other side of Alaska. Aeroplanes were still quite new, so no-one knew if they could fly in such cold weather. Also, Carl Eielson, the only pilot considered skilled enough to manage the flight, was away on a trip at the time. It was therefore agreed that the medicine would be transported using teams of dogs instead.

The trip covered over 1,000 kilometres, most of it along the Iditarod Trail. It took twenty teams just six days to complete the journey. Leonhard Seppala, a Norwegian who had come to Alaska looking for gold, travelled the first 400 of those kilometres. He had to trust his dog Togo's ability to find his way in the blinding snow and Togo turned out to be a reliable guide. The last part of the journey was done by Gunnar Kaasen who had driven dog teams in Alaska for 21 years. His lead dog was Balto. At one point Balto refused to go any further, and saved the team from falling into icy water. The diphtheria was stopped and Balto became a hero.

Nowadays a dog sled race is held every year from Anchorage to Nome, following the route of that famous journey in 1925. It is called the Iditarod and has become known as 'The Last Great Race on Earth'.

Part 4

Question 21–25

Read the text and questions below.
For each question, mark the correct letter **A**, **B**, **C** or **D** on your answer sheet.

Craigie Aitchison

The painter Craigie Aitchison was born in Scotland. He came to London intending to study law, but went to art school instead. There he found the traditional drawing classes difficult, but still kept on painting.

In his late twenties he was given money by the Italian government to study art, and became interested in early Italian artists, which shows in some of his work. He loved the greens and browns of the Italian fields and the clear light there, and wanted to put this light into his paintings.

This led him to paint colours thinly one on top of another from light to dark, but he insists he's never sure what the results will be. He says, 'It's a secret – because I don't know myself. I don't start by painting yellow, knowing I'm going to put anything on top.' Like most talented people, Aitchison makes it sound easy. 'Anyone can do the colours – you can buy them. I simply notice what you put the colours next to.'

Unlike some artists, he never does drawings before he starts a painting, as he feels that if he did, he might get bored and not do the painting afterwards. Instead, Aitchison changes his paintings many times before they are finished. This explains why his favourite models are people who don't ask to see their pictures while he's painting them. 'If I feel they're worried and want to look at the painting, I can't do it.'

Since moving to London years ago, he has not felt part of the Scottish painting scene. He says he is not interested in following any tradition, but just paints the way he can. However, his work still influences young British painters.

21 What is the writer trying to do in the text?

    A   describe particular works by Craigie Aitchison
    B   teach readers how to paint like Craigie Aitchison
    C   introduce readers to the artist Craigie Aitchison
    D   explain how Craigie Aitchison has made money from painting

22 What can the reader learn about Aitchison from the text?

    A   He works in a different way from other artists.
    B   He often gets bored with his paintings.
    C   He improved his drawing by going to art school.
    D   He did some paintings for the Italian government.

23 What does Aitchison say about his use of colour?

    A   He likes starting with the darkest colours first.
    B   He knows the colours he's aiming for when he begins.
    C   He prefers to paint with yellows, greens, and browns.
    D   He understands how different colours work together.

24 Aitchison prefers models who don't

    A   keep talking to him while he's working.
    B   ask him about his strange method of working.
    C   worry about how long the work will take.
    D   feel anxious to see the work as it's developing.

25 What might a visitor at an exhibition say about Aitchison's work?

A
> I love his recent paintings of Scotland, which are very similar to a number of other Scottish painters

B
> You can still see the influence of his trip to Italy in some of these pictures.

C
> You can tell he spent a lot of time drawing the picture before he started painting.

D
> I wonder if his law training helps him at all, especially in selling his work.

Part 5

Questions 26–35

Read the text below and choose the correct word for each space.
For each question, mark the correct letter **A**, **B**, **C** or **D** on your answer sheet.

Example:

| 0 | **A** keep | **B** stay | **C** hold | **D** rest |

Answer:

0	A B C D
	■ ☐ ☐ ☐

ZOOS

People began to **(0)** .... animals in zoos **(26)** .... 3,000 years ago, when the rulers of China opened an enormous zoo called the Gardens of Intelligence. In many of the early zoos, animals **(27)** .... taught to perform for the visitors. This no longer **(28)** .... and it is accepted that the purpose of zoos is for people to see animals behaving naturally.

Today, most cities have a zoo or wildlife park. However, not **(29)** .... approves of zoos. People who think that zoos are a good idea say they **(30)** .... us with the opportunity to **(31)** .... about the natural world and be close to wild animals. Both of **(32)** .... would not be possible **(33)** .... zoos. On the other hand, some people disapprove of zoos because they **(34)** .... it is wrong to put animals in cages, and argue that in zoos which are not **(35)** .... properly, animals live in dirty conditions and eat unsuitable food.

26	**A** above	**B** over	**C** more	**D** beyond
27	**A** are	**B** have	**C** were	**D** had
28	**A** appears	**B** becomes	**C** develops	**D** happens
29	**A** somebody	**B** everybody	**C** nobody	**D** anybody
30	**A** produce	**B** bring	**C** provide	**D** make
31	**A** discover	**B** learn	**C** find	**D** realise
32	**A** that	**B** what	**C** whose	**D** these
33	**A** without	**B** instead	**C** except	**D** unless
34	**A** hope	**B** expect	**C** imagine	**D** believe
35	**A** ordered	**B** managed	**C** decided	**D** aimed

WRITING

Part 1

Questions 1–5

Here are some sentences about a swimming pool.
For each question, complete the second sentence so that it means the same as the first.
Use no more than three words.
Write only the missing words on your answer sheet.
You may use this page for any rough work.

Example:

0   There is a new swimming pool in our town.

Our town .... **a new swimming pool**.

Answer: | **0** | *has got* |

---

1   It's six months since I last went swimming.

I .... **been swimming for six months**.

2   The new pool is near to my home.

It's not .... **the new pool to my home**.

3   If you can't swim, you're not allowed in the deep end.

You're not allowed in the deep end .... **you can swim**.

4   My friend Sam wanted me to go swimming with him.

'Why .... **come swimming with me?' suggested Sam**.

5   I didn't go swimming with Sam because I was very busy.

I was .... **busy to go swimming with Sam**.

Part 2

Question 6

A TV company came to your school yesterday to make a film.

Write an email to your English friend Alice. In your email, you should

- explain why the TV company chose your school
- tell her who or what they filmed
- say when the programme will be shown on television.

Write **35–45 words** on your answer sheet.

Part 3

Write an answer to **one** of the questions (**7** or **8**) in this part.
Write your answer in about **100 words** on your answer sheet.
Mark the question number in the box at the top of your answer sheet.

Question 7

- This is part of a letter you receive from an English friend.

> My parents want me to go on holiday with them this summer but I'd prefer to go somewhere with my friends. I have to choose. What do you think I should do?

- Now write a letter, giving your friend some advice.
- Write your **letter** on your answer sheet.

Question 8

- Your English teacher has asked you to write a story for homework.
- Your story must begin with this sentence:

As soon as I saw the handwriting on the envelope I smiled.

- Write your **story** on your answer sheet.

PAPER 2   LISTENING TEST   approx 35 minutes
(including 6 minutes transfer time)

Part 1

Questions 1–7

There are seven questions in this part.
For each question there are three pictures and a short recording.
Choose the correct picture and put a tick (✓) in the box below it.

Example: How many eggs do you need to make the cake?

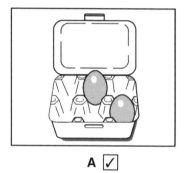

A ✓   B ☐   C ☐

1   Where are the dictionaries?

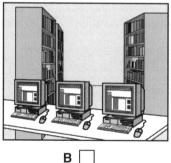

A ☐   B ☐   C ☐

2   Which evening dress does the woman decide to wear?

A ☐   B ☐   C ☐

3 What is the man's job now?

 **A** ☐

 **B** ☐

 **C** ☐

4 Which calendar will the boy buy?

 **A** ☐

 **B** ☐

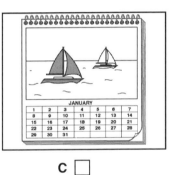 **C** ☐

5 What time will the writer arrive at the bookshop?

 **A** ☐

 **B** ☐

 **C** ☐

6 What did the woman leave in the restaurant?

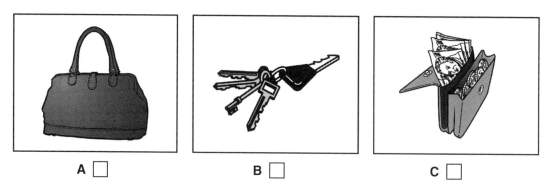

A ☐   B ☐   C ☐

7 Where is the bicycle?

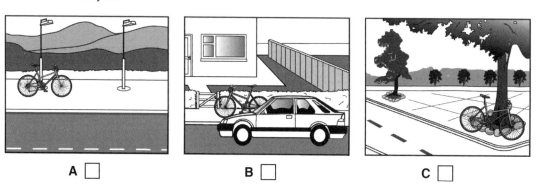

A ☐   B ☐   C ☐

Part 2

Questions 8–13

You will hear a radio interview with Jack Williams, who is talking about a town called Swanton.
For each question, put a tick (✓) in the correct box.

___

8 Where is the town of Swanton located?

    A ☐ near the sea

    B ☐ by a lake

    C ☐ on a hill

9 What does Jack like most about living in Swanton?

    A ☐ There are opportunities for climbing nearby.

    B ☐ There is plenty of activity in the town.

    C ☐ There is interesting wildlife near the town.

10 What does Jack say about entertainment in Swanton?

    A ☐ A music festival takes place in the town.

    B ☐ Its football club has done well this year.

    C ☐ An arts centre has recently opened.

11 Jack is worried about the environment of Swanton because

    A ☐ the water in the river is dirty.

    B ☐ there are few wild birds around today.

    C ☐ pollution has destroyed the plants in one area.

12 What does Jack say about the way
Swanton has changed?

A ☐ He preferred the town when it was
smaller.

B ☐ He thinks it is a more interesting
place.

C ☐ He is sorry that there are fewer jobs
available.

13 Jack is positive about the future of
Swanton because

A ☐ there is a successful new shopping
centre.

B ☐ there will soon be a new airport.

C ☐ a new university is opening.

Part 3

Questions 14–19

You will hear a woman talking on the radio about a singing course she attended.
For each question, fill in the missing information in the numbered space.

Singing for Beginners

Place: Brownstoke College

Course details:

- Lena Phipps, a very good former **(14)** .... singer is the tutor

- the maximum number of students per course is **(15)** ....

- all classes start with exercises that help students to **(16)** ....

- students learn to sing **(17)** .... , modern and pop songs

- accommodation is in single or twin rooms

- cooked breakfast, lunch and dinner are included

- there's a very good lunch, especially **(18)** ....

Date the next course starts: **(19)** .... , 24th September

Part 4

Questions 20–25

Look at the six sentences for this part.
You will hear a conversation between a man, Marco, and his wife, Sarah, about a film they have just seen at the cinema.
Decide if each sentence is correct or incorrect.
If it is correct, put a tick (✓) in the box under **A** for **YES**. If it is not correct, put a tick (✓) in the box under **B** for **NO**.

		A YES	B NO
20	Sarah was expecting to enjoy the film.	☐	☐
21	Marco and Sarah agree that the city in the film was London.	☐	☐
22	Marco feels that the length of the film made it rather boring.	☐	☐
23	Sarah was upset about how some of the audience behaved during the film.	☐	☐
24	Sarah was disappointed with the way the main actor performed.	☐	☐
25	Marco thinks this film is the best the director has made.	☐	☐

About the Speaking test

The Speaking test lasts about 10 to 12 minutes. You take the test with another candidate. There are two examiners in the room. One examiner talks to you and the other examiner listens to you. Both the examiners give you marks.

Part 1

The examiners introduce themselves and then one examiner asks you and your partner to say your names and spell them. This examiner then asks you questions about yourself, your daily life, interests, etc.

Part 2

The examiner asks you to talk about something together and gives you a drawing to help you.

Part 3

You each have a chance to talk by yourselves. The examiner gives you a colour photograph to look at and asks you to talk about it. When you have finished talking, the examiner gives your partner a different photograph to look at and to talk about.

Part 4

The examiner asks you and your partner to say more about the subject of the photographs in Part 3. You may be asked to give your opinion or to talk about something that has happened to you.

Test 3

PAPER 1   READING AND WRITING TEST   (1 hour 30 minutes)

READING

Part 1

Questions 1–5

Look at the text in each question.
What does it say?
Mark the correct letter **A**, **B** or **C** on your answer sheet.

Example:

0

A Do not leave your bicycle touching the window.

B Broken glass may damage your bicycle tyres.

C Your bicycle may not be safe here.

Answer:

1

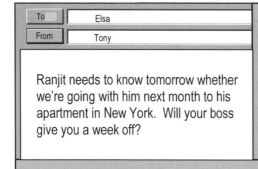

Tony wants Elsa to

A ask her boss for a week's holiday starting tomorrow.

B find out if she can have time off next month.

C go away with him next week for a month.

52

2

CUSTOMERS

If the goods we have delivered are unsatisfactory, call us to arrange collection

A Ring and tell us if you are satisfied with the service we have delivered.

B Telephone us if arrangements for collecting goods are not satisfactory.

C Call us to take the goods back if you are not satisfied with them.

3

Dear Mum
We're staying in the mountains longer than we intended because of storms on the coast. We'll go to the coast before returning home if the weather improves.
Ruth

A Ruth has kept to her plan despite the change in the weather.

B Ruth may not visit the coast if the bad weather continues.

C Ruth intends to leave the mountains early to visit the coast.

4

The food in this container is not suitable for cooking in a microwave oven

A Remove this food from the container before placing in a microwave oven.

B It is advisable to use a suitable container for cooking this food.

C You should avoid putting this food in a microwave oven.

5

Library
Increased charges for borrowing DVDs will be in place from 1st January.

A You will have to pay more to borrow DVDs after 1st January.

B Please return all borrowed DVDs before 1st January.

C There will be additional DVDs to borrow from 1st January.

Part 2

Questions 6–10

The people below all want to hire somewhere for a party or event.
On the opposite page there are descriptions of eight places to hire.
Decide which place would be the most suitable for the following people.
For questions **6–10**, mark the correct letter (**A–H**) on your answer sheet.

6

Jessica is arranging her boss's retirement party. She is looking for somewhere in the town centre that can provide a traditional evening meal for around 100 guests.

7

Amelia is organising her 18th birthday party for 80 friends. She loves to dance and sing along to her favourite tunes. She wants to offer drinks and snacks rather than a sit-down meal.

8

James and Amanda need somewhere to hold their wedding party. They want to be able to take photos outdoors. Most of their 100 guests are coming by car and some will need overnight accommodation.

9

Jens wants to thank his staff of six by taking them out for a day in the countryside. He wants somewhere where they can do lots of fun activities and have a meal.

10

Sophie is organising her company's annual two-day conference. Several meeting rooms are required, one of which must be able to hold 200 people. They will all need to stay one night.

Places to Hire

A Rumbola

Rumbola is available for private bookings of up to 100 people. Hire one of our DJs, who will keep you and your guests moving to the music all night. If you know the words, he'll encourage you to join in! We have no restaurant, but light refreshments are available.

B The Darlington Centre

This modern building, situated in the countryside, is perfect for all business events. We have rooms of varying sizes – the Haversham is the largest with space for 300 people. Included in the price are meals, overnight accommodation and tea/coffee.

C Amazon Café

Situated in the town centre, this restaurant is an exciting place to celebrate a birthday or other special event. The restaurant is decorated to look and sound like a rainforest. Busy and fun, it is popular with young people who like Brazilian food and listening to loud music.

D Sunbury Park

This country house has space for 200 people at events such as weddings and formal dinners. In our beautiful park, we offer a variety of exciting sports and team-building games. As overnight accommodation is not provided, your event will be free from the interruptions often found in a hotel. We have a large car park.

E Narborough Manor

In the historic town centre, this beautiful hotel is the perfect setting for a wedding or birthday party. We can organise entertainment such as magic shows or live music. Lovely paintings and fireplaces make the perfect background for photos. Our dining room seats up to 80.

F Hudsons

This beautiful building dates from 1750 and is the last of its kind in this central location – all around it are shops and businesses. During the day it serves light lunches but in the evening it turns into an old-fashioned, formal restaurant, which can be hired for parties of up to 200 people.

G Hillcourt House

This family-run hotel is famous for its beautiful gardens. It can host private or small business events. The dining room holds 150 and meeting rooms hold 10-20. The hotel is in the countryside but close to two motorways and has plenty of parking spaces.

H Tiger Tom

At weekends, this stylish town-centre restaurant is full of famous faces, but on certain weekdays it can be hired for birthday parties or business events. The menus are modern and it is possible to play your own choice of music while you have your meal.

Part 3

Questions 11–20

Look at the sentences below about a hot-air balloon festival.
Read the text on the opposite page to decide if each sentence is correct or incorrect.
If it is correct, mark **A** on your answer sheet.
If it is not correct, mark **B** on your answer sheet.

---

11   The Albuquerque Balloon Festival lasts over a week.

12   The first festival took place at the opening of the local radio station.

13   The pilots use hand signals to communicate with each other.

14   The 'balloon glow' happens before sunrise and after sunset.

15   Members of the public are forbidden to enter the balloon take-off area.

16   Some advertising balloons join in the festival.

17   You can take a balloon ride to the top of the nearby mountains.

18   You can watch a firework show every evening of the festival.

19   The geography of the area around Albuquerque makes it particularly suitable for ballooning.

20   Visitors should be prepared for a range of temperatures.

The Albuquerque Balloon Festival

Every autumn, the sky above the desert city of Albuquerque in the south-western United States turns into a mass of bright colours. This is the Albuquerque Balloon Festival, an annual nine-day event.

The first festival was held in 1972 to celebrate the 50th birthday of the local radio station. There were about a dozen hot-air balloons and they took off from the car park in the middle of Albuquerque. From these small beginnings, the festival has grown steadily. This year at least a thousand balloons from over one third of the countries of the world are expected at its current out-of-town site.

What to see
The pilots are in radio contact with each other and all light up the burners of their balloons at the same time. These are known as 'balloon glows' and are an opportunity to take fantastic photographs. However, you must arrive just after night has fallen or before 5.30 am to see these 'glows' as the balloons rise into the dark sky.

During the day, you can walk around among the balloons and chat to the pilots as they prepare for take-off. The balloons come in all sizes and colours, some in the shapes of animals or cartoon characters – and, of course, well-known products such as varieties of soft drinks and fast food. Kids will love it.

In the afternoon, why not take to the sky yourself by arranging a balloon flight over the desert with one of the many companies offering balloon rides? Another possibility is to take the cable car from the desert floor to the top of the nearby mountains, the longest such ride anywhere, and enjoy a bird's-eye view of the festival. There are plenty of other attractions for visitors of all ages, including balloon races and firework displays on the opening evening and the last three evenings of the festival.

The Albuquerque Box
This is a local wind pattern that creates perfect conditions for balloonists. The Sandia Mountains protect the balloons from strong winds, and at the same time create gentler currents of wind at different heights. This means that by rising or descending, skilful pilots can control the direction of their balloons.

Practical advice
Buy your tickets in advance (they are available online) and save yourself a long wait to get into the festival site. Wear several layers of thin clothing. At night and in the early morning it can be quite cool, but during the day sunglasses and suncream are essential. Bring a flashlight for night-time events and, of course, bring your camera. If you're not a digital photographer, you'll need high-speed film for evening and night-time pictures.

Part 4

Questions 21–25

Read the text and questions below.
For each question, mark the correct letter **A**, **B**, **C** or **D** on your answer sheet.

The Young Achiever of the Year

Kal Kaur Rai has always been interested in fashion and has just won the
title of *Young Achiever of the Year* at the Asian Business Awards. Ever since
she was a child, she has drawn clothes and designed patterns. She never
told her hard-working parents, who own a supermarket, that she wanted to
turn her hobby into a career. She thought they expected her to go into a
more established business, so she went to university to do a management
degree.

After university, she moved to London and worked in an advertising agency. She had to
attend industry events but couldn't afford the designer clothes she liked. She started making
skirts and tops for herself. When her friends saw her clothes, they asked her to make things
for them. She then found a small shop in London willing to take her designs on a sale-or-
return basis. They were very popular and nothing came back. This encouraged her to leave
her advertising job, take out a £20,000 loan and begin her own womenswear label.

Kal's parents were not angry about her career change and said they would support her, which
really pleased her. Her clothes are now on sale in over 70 stores and her business has an
income of over £500,000. Her clothes appear in fashion magazines, she designs for pop stars
and she has just gained public recognition by winning this award. Her business has come a
long way and she knows she is extremely lucky. 'What I do is my hobby – and I get paid for it!
But remember, I've worked hard for this.'

21   What is the writer trying to do in the text?

    A   encourage fashion designers to make better business plans
    B   compare a job in fashion with other choices of career
    C   give details of recent changes in the fashion industry
    D   explain how a woman set up a fashion business

22   What does the reader learn about Kal's parents?

    A   They wanted Kal to help them run the family business.
    B   They did not realise that Kal wanted to work in fashion.
    C   They insisted Kal should continue with her job in advertising.
    D   They did not think Kal worked hard enough at university.

23 Kal decided to borrow £20,000 when

    A   all her clothes in the London shop were sold.

    B   her friends asked her to make clothes for them.

    C   she lost her job at the advertising agency.

    D   the fashion industry was in a period of growth.

24 What does Kal say about her career?

    A   She plans to open more stores.

    B   She believes that she deserves her success.

    C   She particularly enjoys designing for famous people.

    D   She expects more people to buy her clothes after the award.

25 What might Kal say now about her career?

A
My management degree has helped me more than anything else. It's so important that young people interested in fashion can deal with money.

B
I've learnt so much working for other fashion designers. Without this experience, I couldn't have started my own business.

C
Running a fashion business is a dream come true and my parents being happy with my choice makes it even more special.

D
Even when I was at university, my friends liked the clothes I made. This encouraged me to think about a career in fashion.

Part 5

Questions 26–35

Read the text below and choose the correct word for each space.
For each question, mark the correct letter **A**, **B**, **C** or **D** on your answer sheet.

Example:

0	**A** in	**B** on	**C** at	**D** from

Answer:

0	A	B	C	D
	▬	☐	☐	☐

Sweden's Ice Hotel

The village of Jukkasjärvi is **(0)** .... Swedish Lapland, and winter temperatures there can reach −40° C. But 6,000 holidaymakers **(26)** .... go there annually, to visit what is probably Europe's most unusual accommodation.

In this hotel you eat, drink, and sleep in rooms made **(27)** .... ice. If you want, you can **(28)** .... get married in one. The bar is ice too, and putting hot drinks on it is obviously not **(29)** .... ! The bedrooms are around −4° C, but fortunately guests are **(30)** .... with special sleeping bags that will keep **(31)** .... warm in the coldest of temperatures. **(32)** .... outdoor clothes can be supplied too, if needed.

The hotel is never more than six months old **(33)** .... it melts in summer, and **(34)** .... winter it is rebuilt. Creating the hotel **(35)** .... 10,000 tonnes of ice, plus 30,000 tonnes of snow.

26	**A** therefore	**B** ever	**C** also	**D** still
27	**A** by	**B** of	**C** within	**D** for
28	**A** even	**B** however	**C** already	**D** yet
29	**A** supported	**B** recognised	**C** recommended	**D** agreed
30	**A** given	**B** offered	**C** provided	**D** delivered
31	**A** these	**B** those	**C** they	**D** them
32	**A** Suitable	**B** Convenient	**C** Acceptable	**D** Satisfactory
33	**A** although	**B** because	**C** so	**D** while
34	**A** other	**B** any	**C** each	**D** another
35	**A** brings	**B** puts	**C** fetches	**D** takes

WRITING

PART 1

Questions 1–5

Here are some sentences about a well-known painting, *La Gioconda* (or *Mona Lisa*).
For each question, complete the second sentence so that it means the same as the first.
Use no more than three words.
Write only the missing words on your answer sheet.
You may use this page for any rough work.

Example:

0   It was 1503 when Leonardo da Vinci started to paint *La Gioconda*.

Leonardo da Vinci started to paint *La Gioconda* .... **1503**.

Answer:	0	in

---

1   Probably, no other painting is as famous as *La Gioconda*.

La Gioconda is probably .... **painting in the world**.

2   Nobody is sure of the identity of the woman in the painting.

Nobody is sure .... **the woman in the painting is**.

3   People find the smile of the woman in the painting interesting.

People are .... **in the smile of the woman in the painting**.

4   It took Leonardo a long time to paint this picture.

Leonardo spent a long time .... **this picture**.

5   Does anyone know what this picture is worth today?

Does anyone know how .... **this picture is worth today?**

Part 2

Question 6

You arranged to meet your English friend Sally next Tuesday, but you have to change the time.

Write an email to Sally. In your email, you should

- suggest a new time to meet on Tuesday
- explain why you need to change the time
- remind Sally where you arranged to meet.

Write **35–45 words** on your answer sheet.

Part 3

Write an answer to **one** of the questions (**7** or **8**) in this part.
Write your answer in about **100 words** on your answer sheet.
Mark the question number in the box at the top of your answer sheet.

Question 7

- Your Scottish penfriend has written to you for advice.

> Next month, I'm moving with my family to a different area. I have
> to choose between going to a small school in the countryside or
> a large school in the centre of town. What should I do?

- Now write a letter to your penfriend, giving your advice.
- Write your **letter** on your answer sheet.

Question 8

- Your English teacher has asked you to write a story.
- Your story must begin with this sentence:

As the man left the café, Maria saw that his phone was still on the table.

- Write your **story** on your answer sheet.

PAPER 2   LISTENING TEST   approx 35 minutes
(including 6 minutes transfer time)

Part 1

Questions 1–7

There are seven questions in this part.
For each question there are three pictures and a short recording.
Choose the correct picture and put a tick (✓) in the box below it.

Example: How did the woman get to work?

A ☑   B ☐   C ☐

1   What regular exercise does David do at the moment?

 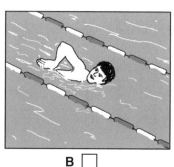 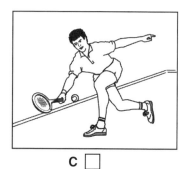

A ☐   B ☐   C ☐

2   What should Suzie take to Emma's house?

 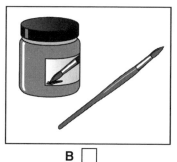 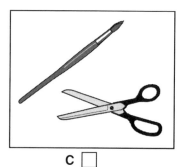

A ☐   B ☐   C ☐

3   Which kind of T-shirt did the boy choose?

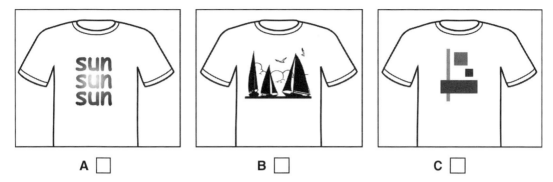

A ☐   B ☐   C ☐

4   What frightened the man?

A ☐   B ☐   C ☐

5   Where is the man calling from?

A ☐   B ☐   C ☐

6   How did the woman spend her last holiday?

A ☐   B ☐   C ☐

7   Where is the girl's purse?

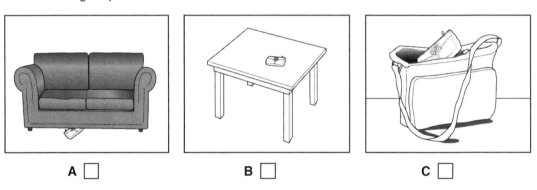

A ☐   B ☐   C ☐

Part 2

Questions 8–13

You will hear a radio interview with a ballet dancer called Elena Karpov, who is talking about her life and career.
For each question, put a tick (✓) in the correct box.

---

8 Elena decided to become a dancer when she was

    A ☐ seven.

    B ☐ nine.

    C ☐ eleven.

9 At ballet school in New York, Elena

    A ☐ was the only student from Bulgaria.

    B ☐ found learning the language hard.

    C ☐ learned to be independent.

10 What does Elena say about the ballet called *Cinderella*?

    A ☐ Children will enjoy it.

    B ☐ The music was unfamiliar to her.

    C ☐ She saw it when she was a child.

11 In her free time, Elena likes to

    A ☐ go sightseeing.

    B ☐ go to clubs.

    C ☐ go shopping.

12   What does Elena often do for her fans?

    A ☐ She gives them a flower.

    B ☐ She signs one of her photographs.

    C ☐ She sends them a free ticket.

13   What does Elena like best about her job?

    A ☐ appearing on television

    B ☐ doing something she loves

    C ☐ travelling to different countries

Part 3

Questions 14–19

You will hear a group leader talking to some students who are going to visit an important athletics event in Birmingham.
For each question, fill in the missing information in the numbered space.

Athletics Championships

Date of college trip: **(14)** 15th ....

Number of sportspeople who will compete: **(15)** ....

How the group will travel to Birmingham: by **(16)** ....

What group members should take on the day: **(17)** ....

Name of the website page: **(18)** ....

Which day other details will be available to students: **(19)** ....

Part 4

Questions 20–25

Look at the six sentences for this part.
You will hear two friends, a boy, Rolf, and a girl, Maria, talking about the jobs they would like to do in the future.
Decide if each sentence is correct or incorrect.
If it is correct, put a tick (✓) in the box under **A** for **YES**. If it is not correct, put a tick (✓) in the box under **B** for **NO**.

		A YES	B NO
20	Maria would like to travel a lot as part of her job.	☐	☐
21	Maria is confident she will be able to work for an airline.	☐	☐
22	Rolf intends to do a job connected with his degree.	☐	☐
23	Maria and Rolf agree it is important to have a good salary.	☐	☐
24	Maria hopes to work for several different employers.	☐	☐
25	Rolf's ambition is to manage his own company one day.	☐	☐

About the Speaking test

The Speaking test lasts about 10 to 12 minutes. You take the test with another candidate. There are two examiners in the room. One examiner talks to you and the other examiner listens to you. Both the examiners give you marks.

Part 1

The examiners introduce themselves and then one examiner asks you and your partner to say your names and spell them. This examiner then asks you questions about yourself, your daily life, interests, etc.

Part 2

The examiner asks you to talk about something together and gives you a drawing to help you.

Part 3

You each have a chance to talk by yourselves. The examiner gives you a colour photograph to look at and asks you to talk about it. When you have finished talking, the examiner gives your partner a different photograph to look at and to talk about.

Part 4

The examiner asks you and your partner to say more about the subject of the photographs in Part 3. You may be asked to give your opinion or to talk about something that has happened to you.

Test 4

PAPER 1   READING AND WRITING TEST   (1 hour 30 minutes)

READING

Part 1

Questions 1–5

Look at the text in each question.
What does it say?
Mark the correct letter **A**, **B** or **C** on your answer sheet.

Example:

0

A Valuable objects are removed at night.

B Valuables should not be left in the van.

C This van is locked at night.

Answer:

1
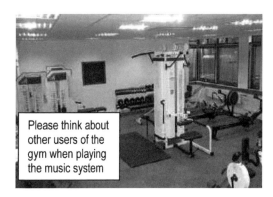

A The members of the gym think the music system is very useful.

B When using the music system in the gym, please remember to switch it off.

C If you put on some music, consider the other people in the gym.

2

> Having a great time.
> Some of the group
> have returned home,
> but the rest of us are
> having a boat trip
> tomorrow.
> See you next week.

The writer is

A going home with the rest of the group tomorrow.

B going on a boat with members of the group tomorrow.

C going out with the whole group tomorrow.

3

English Library

All books are arranged
in A-Z order.
Please put them back
correctly

A You should return your books to the assistant in the correct order.

B The books are easy to find because they are all arranged by level.

C You should replace books in the order that you found them.

4

*If entrance
door is locked,
please press
button to
contact hotel
reception.*

A Use this button to call hotel staff if you cannot get in.

B If you cannot lock the door, please contact hotel reception.

C Press this button to unlock the entrance door.

5

> David
> I'll be back late. Don't
> forget Carla needs a lift
> to band practice at
> school – please make
> sure she's in uniform.
> Marta

What should David do?

A He should remind Carla that someone is picking her up for band practice.

B He should check Carla is dressed properly and take her to band practice.

C He should make Carla practise before she goes to her school band meeting.

Part 2

Questions 6–10

The people below are all on holiday in the north of England and want to go for a walk in the countryside.

On the opposite page there are descriptions of eight country walks.

Decide which walk would be the most suitable for the following people.

For questions **6–10** mark the correct letter (**A–H**) on your answer sheet.

---

6  Mary and George, a retired couple, want to go on a short walk that lasts about an hour. They like old houses and pretty countryside, but can't climb steep hills.

7  The Thompson family want to spend a day out, including lunch. The parents like visiting gardens, but aren't interested in country houses. The two children are very active and like animals.

8  Carolina and Juan are experienced, independent walkers. They would like a long walk followed by a meal in a pub. Although they like attractive old villages, they don't enjoy crowded places.

9  Kenzo would like to join an organised walk to learn about the area. He is interested in history and wants to see one of the best-known places in this part of the country.

10  Belinda and her young teenage son Tom both enjoy being outdoors. Belinda wants to go walking and then find a nice café to relax in. Tom gets bored just walking and prefers other activities, especially sports.

Country Walks

A Lime House and Country Park

The house attracts thousands of visitors, but this is a pleasant walk (for the fit!) away from the crowds, through parkland, woods and up onto the hills. Popular with bird-watchers. Allow three hours. The house was built in 1570. Gardens closed to the public; information centre, café and souvenir shop open daily.

B Howden Lake

This two-hour walk attracts thousands of visitors. When the water is low, you can see a village which was flooded 300 years ago. Quiet café with beautiful views. Children can go sailing and windsurfing on the lake with trained instructors.

C Devonshire Park

Take a really enjoyable walk in the countryside surrounding the park. Allow at least half a day, or make it a full day by visiting the adventure playground and farmyard (both great for young children). Stop at the café (open all day) or enjoy the fantastic gardens, with beautiful fountains. Guided walks available for small groups.

D Stanton

This walk is definitely for very fit walkers only – the tracks get very slippery after rain. Allow six hours and start early! You're unlikely to meet another person all day. Fantastic views of farmland in the valleys below. Be sure to pack sandwiches – you'll be up on the hilltops all day.

E Hope Village

A leisurely way to spend an hour or two is by visiting the busy village of Hope with its lovely old cottages, traditional pubs and country gardens. A gentle walk towards the hills will soon bring you to superb views.

F Strines

You need to be used to walking to successfully complete this seven-hour walk through the wildest scenery in the area. Follow a little-known footpath to the highest point for miles. The traditional pub down in the village serves hot food from 12.00 daily.

G Cornford

This is an easy walk through a little-known valley beside clear streams with woodland flowers, birds and animals. See the 200-year-old buildings from the cloth-making industry which now stand empty. Private tours can be arranged. Allow half a day for the walk.

H Langsett

After a steep climb, this is an exciting walk along easy paths, which are crowded at weekends (people come from all over Britain to climb Langsett). The views are dramatic, and it's a popular place for family picnics. Guided walks start from the nearby village (10 am Sundays) and visit 800-year-old woodland and ruins dating back two thousand years.

Part 3

Questions 11–20

Look at the sentences below about a competition.
Read the text on the opposite page to decide if each sentence is correct or incorrect.
If it is correct, mark **A** on your answer sheet.
If it is not correct, mark **B** on your answer sheet.

11   All prize winners will have their stories printed in the magazine *Keep Writing*.

12   Most people entering the competition last year followed the advice they were given.

13   Writers should remember to check that any information they use is correct.

14   The magazine is looking for stories which have an unexpected ending.

15   Writers are encouraged to describe the people in their stories clearly.

16   Stories should either be written clearly by hand or typed.

17   Late entries can be faxed if necessary.

18   The magazine will send back all stories which have failed to be selected.

19   The rules of the competition are different this year from last year.

20   Writers can enter stories which magazines outside Britain have already printed.

Write a winning story!

You could win £1,000 in this year's Fiction Prize and have your story printed in Keep Writing magazine. Ten other lucky people will win a cheque for £100.

Once again, we need people who can write good stories. The judges, who include Mary Littlejohn, the novelist, Michael Brown, the television reporter, and Susan Hitchins, *Keep Writing's* editor, are looking for interesting and original stories. Detective fiction was extremely popular last year, although the competition winner produced a love story. You can write about whatever you want but here's some advice to start you thinking:

- **Write about what you know**

This is the advice which every writer should pay attention to and, last year, nearly everyone who wrote for us did exactly that. Love, family, problems with friends – these were the main subjects of the stories. However, you need to turn ordinary situations into something interesting that people will want to read about. Make the reader want to continue reading by writing about ordinary things in a new and surprising way.

- **Get your facts right**

It's no good giving a description of a town or explaining how a jet engine works if you get it wrong. So avoid writing anything unless you're certain about it.

- **Hold the reader's attention**

Make the beginning interesting and the ending a surprise. There is nothing worse than a poor ending. Develop the story carefully and try to think of something unusual happening at the end.

- **Think about the characters**

Try to bring the people in your story alive for the reader by using well-chosen words to make them seem real.

Your story must be your own work, between 2,000 and 2,500 words and typed, double-spaced, on one side only of each sheet of paper.

Even if you're in danger of missing the closing date, we are unable to accept stories by fax or email. You must include the application form with your story. Unfortunately your story cannot be returned, nor can we discuss our decisions.

You should not have had any fiction printed in any magazine or book in this country – a change in the rules by popular request – and the story must not have appeared in print or in recorded form, for example on radio or TV, anywhere in the world.

Your fee of £5 will go to the Writers' Association. Make your cheque payable to *Keep Writing* and send it with the application form and your story to:

Keep Writing
75 Broad Street
Birmingham
B12 4TG

The closing date is 30 July and we will inform the winner within one month of this date. Please note that if you win, you must agree to have your story printed in our magazine.

Part 4

Questions 21–25

Read the text and questions below.
For each question, mark the correct letter **A**, **B**, **C** or **D** on your answer sheet.

Being an older student

At 32, I have just finished my first year at university. As well as attending lectures regularly, I have had to learn to read books quickly and write long essays.

I decided to go to university after fourteen years away from the classroom. As a secretary, although I was earning a reasonable amount of money, I was bored doing something where I hardly had to think. I became more and more depressed by the idea that I was stuck in the job. I was jealous of the students at the local university, who looked happy, carefree and full of hope, and part of something that I wanted to explore further.

However, now that I've actually become a student I find it hard to mix with younger colleagues. They are always mistaking me for a lecturer and asking me questions I can't answer. I also feel separated from the lecturers because, although we are the same age, I know so much less than them. But I am glad of this opportunity to study because I know you need a qualification to get a rewarding job, which is really important to me. Unlike most eighteen-year-olds, I much prefer a weekend with my books to one out partying. Then there are the normal student benefits of long holidays and theatre and cinema discounts. I often have doubts about what I'll do after university, but I hope that continuing my education at this late date has been a wise choice.

21   What is the writer trying to do in the text?

    A   help lecturers understand older students
    B   explain her reasons for returning to study
    C   suggest some good methods for studying
    D   complain about the attitude of young students

22   What can a reader find out about the writer from this text?

    A   when she left school
    B   how long her university course is
    C   where she will work in future
    D   what subject she is studying

23 How did the writer feel about her job as a secretary?

    A   Her salary wasn't good enough.
    B   It gave her the opportunity to study.
    C   It didn't make use of her brain.
    D   Her colleagues made her depressed.

24 In her spare time, the writer likes to

    A   go out to parties.
    B   earn some money.
    C   travel a lot.
    D   do extra study.

25 Which of these sentences describes the writer?

A

> She realises the value of a university degree.

B

> She gets on well with the other students.

C

> She is confident about the future.

D

> She finds university life easier than she expected.

Part 5

Questions 26–35

Read the text below and choose the correct word for each space.
For each question, mark the correct letter **A**, **B**, **C** or **D** on your answer sheet.

Example:

| 0 | **A** on | **B** of | **C** to | **D** out |

Answer:

0	A B C D
	■ □ □ □

Henry Ford

Henry Ford was born **(0)** .... a farm in Michigan in 1863 but he did not like farming. When he was fifteen he began work as a mechanic and in 1893 he built his first car. After he **(26)** .... driven it 1,500 kilometres, he sold it and built two bigger cars. Then, in 1903, he **(27)** .... the Ford Motor Company. By **(28)** .... strong but light steel, he built cheap cars for **(29)** .... people to buy. In 1908, he built the first Ford Model 'T', **(30)** .... sold for $825. He was soon selling 100 cars **(31)** .... day. By 1927, the Ford Motor Company was **(32)** .... $700 million. Early Ford cars were simple and cheap, but **(33)** .... things simple sometimes **(34)** .... less choice. 'You **(35)** .... have any colour you like,' said Henry Ford of the Model T, 'as long as it's black.'

26	**A** is	**B** was	**C** had	**D** has
27	**A** raised	**B** started	**C** led	**D** appeared
28	**A** putting	**B** operating	**C** using	**D** managing
29	**A** usual	**B** ordinary	**C** general	**D** typical
30	**A** where	**B** which	**C** who	**D** what
31	**A** a	**B** some	**C** the	**D** one
32	**A** rich	**B** worth	**C** expensive	**D** dear
33	**A** remaining	**B** staying	**C** keeping	**D** holding
34	**A** meant	**B** decided	**C** planned	**D** intended
35	**A** will	**B** ought	**C** need	**D** can

Visual material for the Speaking test

1A

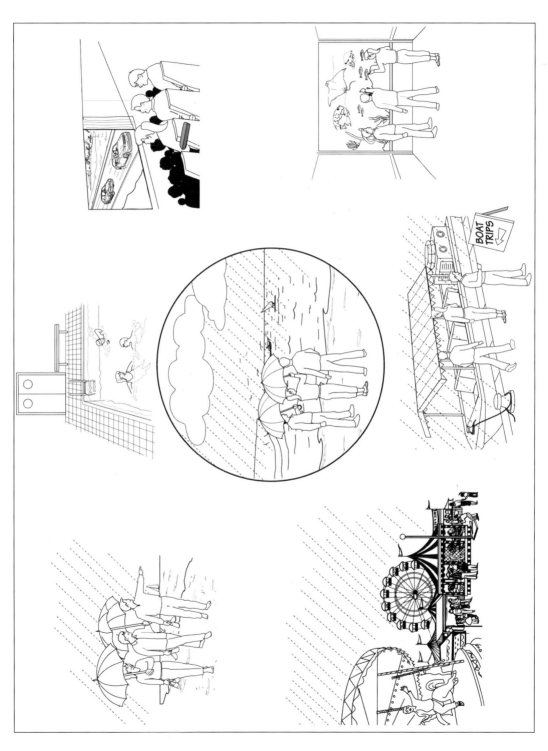

Visual material for the Speaking test

1B

2C

II

2A

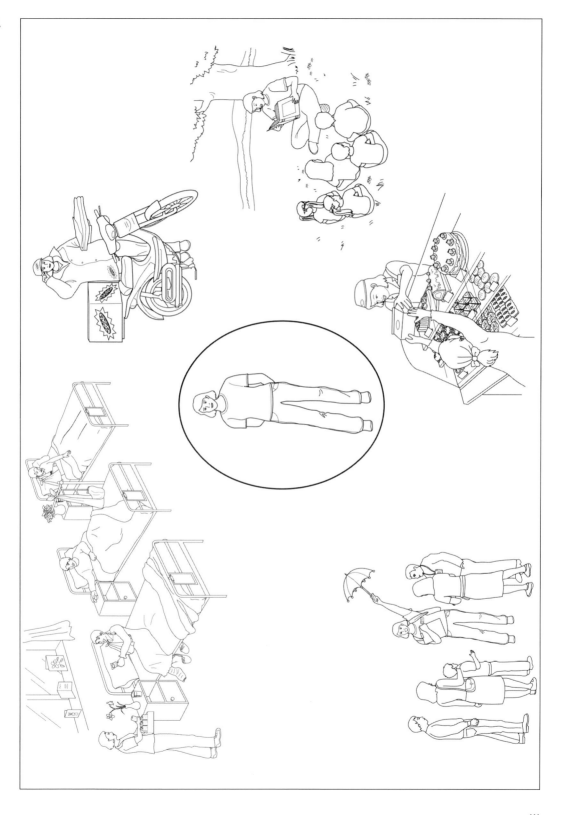

Visual material for the Speaking test

2B

1C

IV

3A

3B

4C

4A

4B

3C

WRITING

Part 1

Questions 1–5

Here are some sentences about a school trip to a museum.
For each question, complete the second sentence so that it means the same as the first.
Use no more than three words.
Write only the missing words on your answer sheet.
You may use this page for any rough work.

Example:

0   Mr Winters told the class they were going to visit the museum.

   Mr Winters said to the class, '... **to visit the museum.'**

Answer: | 0 | *We're going* |

---

1   The museum was near the school.

   The museum was not .... **the school**.

2   It cost £3 to visit the museum.

   They had to .... **£3 to visit the museum**.

3   The class was taken around the museum by a guide.

   A museum guide .... **around the museum**.

4   They did not leave until 4 o'clock.

   It was 4 o'clock .... **they left the museum**.

5   Everybody thought that the museum visit was boring.

   Everybody was .... **by the museum visit**.

Part 2

Question 6

Your friend Alex has invited you to go to the cinema tomorrow, but you can't go.

Write an email to Alex. In your email, you should

- apologise
- explain why you can't go
- invite Alex to do something with you another day.

Write **35–45 words** on your answer sheet.

Part 3

Write an answer to **one** of the questions (**7** or **8**) in this part.
Write your answer in about **100 words** on your answer sheet.
Mark the question number in the box at the top of your answer sheet.

Question 7

- This is part of a letter you receive from an English friend.

> We had dinner at a new restaurant yesterday. It was great! How often do you eat out? What's your favourite restaurant like?

- Now write a letter, answering your friend's questions.
- Write your **letter** on your answer sheet.

Question 8

- Your English teacher has asked you to write a story.
- Your story must begin with this sentence:

I had a real surprise when I turned on the television.

- Write your **story** on your answer sheet.

PAPER 2   LISTENING TEST   approx 35 minutes
(including 6 minutes transfer time)

Part 1

Questions 1–7

There are seven questions in this part.
For each question there are three pictures and a short recording.
Choose the correct picture and put a tick (✓) in the box below it.

Example: How did the woman get to work?

A ✓   B ☐   C ☐

---

1   What did the thieves steal?

A ☐   B ☐   C ☐

2   What present will they take?

A ☐   B ☐   C ☐

3   What will the woman eat tonight?

A ☐   B ☐   C ☐

4   How much will the girl's ticket cost?

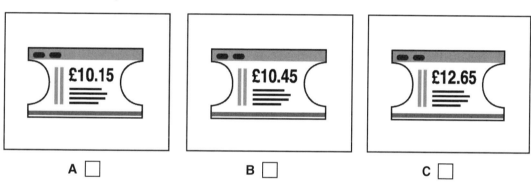

A ☐   B ☐   C ☐

5   What is the grandmother's job now?

A ☐   B ☐   C ☐

6 Which button has the boy lost?

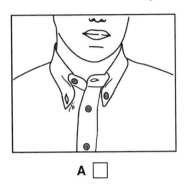 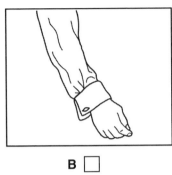 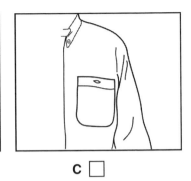

A ☐   **B** ☐   **C** ☐

7 What will the man do first?

A ☐   **B** ☐   **C** ☐

Part 2

Questions 8–13

You will hear Sarah Brown talking about her work as a television weather forecaster.
For each question put a tick (✓) in the correct box.

8   How long has Sarah worked as a weather
    forecaster?

A ☐ two years

B ☐ seven years

C ☐ thirty years

9   What does Sarah say about her job?

A ☐ She sometimes has to work at night.

B ☐ She enjoys getting up early.

C ☐ She works ten or twelve hours
      a day.

10   When Sarah does a weather forecast,

A ☐ she prepares it in advance.

B ☐ she sometimes forgets her words.

C ☐ she worries about making a
      mistake.

11   Sarah's husband

A ☐ works on the same days each week.

B ☐ wants to move nearer his work.

C ☐ spends a lot of time travelling.

12 Sarah is pleased because she

A ☐ has got her pilot's licence.

B ☐ taught her husband to play tennis.

C ☐ took part in a long race.

13 A man in India wanted

A ☐ to meet Sarah's family.

B ☐ a photo of Sarah.

C ☐ to receive a letter from Sarah.

Part 3

Questions 14–19

You will hear a radio talk about holidays in Northumberland.
For each question fill in the missing information in the numbered space.

Holidays in Northumberland

Useful Information

- Read Peter Green's book called '**(14)** .... *around Northumberland* '.
- Lots of things to see, for example **(15)** ....
- Accommodation in flats, hotels, cottages or bed and breakfast places.
- Best time to go is **(16)** ....

Bike Hire

- One week – £35
- Two weeks – **(17)** £ ....

Local Events

- June – *Food Festival*
- August – *International Festival of* **(18)** ....

National Park Activities

- Guided walks
- Photography
- **(19)** ....

Part 4

Questions 20–25

Look at the six sentences for this part.
You will hear a conversation between a girl called Julia and her father, about choosing a course at university.
Decide if each sentence is correct or incorrect.
If it is correct, put a tick (✓) in the box under **A** for **YES**. If it is not correct, put a tick (✓) in the box under **B** for **NO**.

		A YES	B NO
20	Julia wants to choose a course as soon as possible.	☐	☐
21	Julia's father thinks that studying business may be boring.	☐	☐
22	Julia's father believes Julia's friend is making the wrong choice.	☐	☐
23	Julia's father thinks she might find studying business too difficult.	☐	☐
24	Julia is confident about her maths.	☐	☐
25	Julia is keen to consider her father's suggestion.	☐	☐

About the Speaking test

The Speaking test lasts about 10 to 12 minutes. You take the test with another candidate. There are two examiners in the room. One examiner talks to you and the other examiner listens to you. Both the examiners give you marks.

Part 1

The examiners introduce themselves and then one examiner asks you and your partner to say your names and spell them. This examiner then asks you questions about yourself, your daily life, interests, etc.

Part 2

The examiner asks you to talk about something together and gives you a drawing to help you.

Part 3

You each have a chance to talk by yourselves. The examiner gives you a colour photograph to look at and asks you to talk about it. When you have finished talking, the examiner gives your partner a different photograph to look at and to talk about.

Part 4

The examiner asks you and your partner to say more about the subject of the photographs in Part 3. You may be asked to give your opinion or to talk about something that has happened to you.

Frames for the Speaking test

TEST 1

Part 1 (2–3 minutes)

Tasks   Identifying oneself; giving information about oneself; talking about interests.

Phase 1
Examiner

A/B   Good morning / afternoon / evening.
Can I have your mark sheets, please?

A/B   I'm ………… and this is ………… .
He / she is just going to listen to us.

A   Now, what's your name?
Thank you.

B   And what's your name?
Thank you.

B Candidate B, what's your surname? How do you spell it? Thank you.	How do you write your family / second name?
A And, Candidate A, what's your surname? How do you spell it? Thank you.	How do you write your family / second name?

(Ask the following questions. Use candidates' names throughout. Ask Candidate A first.) Where do you live / come from? *Adult students* Do you work or are you a student in . . .? What do you do / study? *School-age students* Do you study English at school? Do you like it? Thank you. *(Repeat for Candidate B.)*	 Do you live in . . .? Have you got a job? What job do you do? / What subject(s) do you study? Do you have English lessons?

Phase 2
Examiner
(Select one or more questions from the list to ask each candidate. Ask Candidate B first.)

	Back-up prompts
Do you enjoy studying English? Why (not)?	Do you like studying English?
Do you think that English will be useful for you in the future?	Will you use English in the future?
What did you do yesterday evening / last weekend?	Did you do anything yesterday evening / last weekend? What?
What do you enjoy doing in your free time?	What do you like to do in your free time?

Thank you.

(Introduction to Part 2)

In the next part, you are going to talk to each other.

Part 2 (2–3 minutes)

A RAINY DAY

Tasks   Discussing alternatives; expressing opinions; making choices.

Examiner   *Say to both candidates*:

I'm going to describe a situation to you.

A group of friends is planning to spend a day by the sea, but when they arrive it's raining. Talk together about the different things they can do while it's raining, and then decide which will be most interesting.

Here is a picture with some ideas to help you.

Ask both candidates to look at picture 1A on page I of the Student's Book and repeat the frame.

I'll say that again.

A group of friends is planning to spend a day by the sea, but when they arrive it's raining. Talk together about the different things they can do while it's raining, and then decide which will be most interesting.

All right? Talk together.

Allow the candidates enough time to complete the task without intervention. Prompt only if necessary.

Part 3 (3 minutes)

TAKING A BREAK

Tasks   Describing people and places; saying where people and things are and what different people are doing.

Examiner   *Say to both candidates*:

> Now, I'd like each of you to talk on your own about something. I'm going to give each of you a photograph of people taking a break.
>
> Candidate A, here is your photograph. *(Ask Candidate A to look at photo 1B on page II of the Student's Book.)* Please show it to Candidate B, but I'd like you to talk about it. Candidate B, you just listen. I'll give you your photograph in a moment.
>
> Candidate A, please tell us what you can see in your photograph.

(Candidate A)   *Approximately one minute*

If there is a need to intervene, prompts rather than direct questions should be used.

Ask Candidate A to close his/her book.

Examiner   Now, Candidate B, here is your photograph. It also shows someone taking a break. *(Ask Candidate B to look at photo 1C on page IV of the Student's Book.)* Please show it to Candidate A and tell us what you can see in the photograph.

(Candidate B)   *Approximately one minute*

Ask the candidates to close their books before moving to Part 4.

Part 4 (3 minutes)

Tasks   Talking about one's likes and dislikes; expressing opinions: talking about habits.

Examiner   *Say to both candidates*:

> Your photographs showed people taking a break. Now, I'd like you to talk together about when you take a break during the day, and where you like to go during your break.

Allow the candidates enough time to complete the task without intervention. Prompt only if necessary.

> **Back-up prompts**
> 1. Talk about **when** you take a break.
> 2. Talk about **where** you like to **go** for your break.
> 3. Talk about what you **do** during your break.
> 4. Talk about **why** it's **important** to take a break.

> Thank you. That's the end of the test.

TEST 2

Part 1 (2–3 minutes)

Tasks   Identifying oneself; giving information about oneself; talking about interests.

Phase 1
Examiner

A/B   Good morning / afternoon / evening.
          Can I have your mark sheets, please?

A/B   I'm ………… and this is ………… .
          He / she is just going to listen to us.

A   Now, what's your name?
          Thank you.

B   And what's your name?
          Thank you.

Back-up prompts

B Candidate B, what's your surname? How do you spell it? Thank you.	How do you write your family / second name?
A And, Candidate A, what's your surname? How do you spell it? Thank you.	How do you write your family / second name?

(Ask the following questions. Use candidates' names throughout. Ask Candidate A first.) Where do you live / come from? <u>Adult students</u> Do you work or are you a student in . . .? What do you do / study? <u>School-age students</u> Do you study English at school? Do you like it? Thank you. *(Repeat for Candidate B.)*	Do you live in . . .? Have you got a job? What job do you do? / What subject(s) do you study? Do you have English lessons?

Frames for the Speaking test

Phase 2
Examiner

(Select one or more questions from the list to ask each candidate. Ask Candidate B first.)

	Back-up prompts
Do you enjoy studying English? Why (not)?	Do you like studying English?
Do you think that English will be useful for you in the future?	Will you use English in the future?
What did you do yesterday evening / last weekend?	Did you do anything yesterday evening / last weekend? What?
What do you enjoy doing in your free time?	What do you like to do in your free time?

Thank you.

(Introduction to Part 2)

In the next part, you are going to talk to each other.

Part 2 (2–3 minutes)

MEETING PEOPLE

Tasks   Discussing alternatives; expressing opinions; making choices.

Examiner   *Say to both candidates:*

> I'm going to describe a situation to you.
>
> A student you know wants a summer job where she can meet new people. Talk together about the jobs she could do and then decide which would be best for meeting new people.
>
> Here is a picture with some ideas to help you.

Ask both candidates to look at picture 2A on page III of the Student's Book and repeat the frame.

> I'll say that again.
>
> A student you know wants a summer job where she can meet new people. Talk together about the jobs she could do and then decide which would be best for meeting new people.
>
> All right? Talk together.

Allow the candidates enough time to complete the task without intervention. Prompt only if necessary.

Part 3 (3 minutes)

RELAXING AT HOME

Tasks   Describing people and places; saying where people and things are and what different people are doing.

Examiner   *Say to both candidates*:

> Now, I'd like each of you to talk on your own about something. I'm going to give each of you a photograph of people relaxing at home.
>
> Candidate A, here is your photograph. *(Ask Candidate A to look at photo 2B on page IV of the Student's Book.)* Please show it to Candidate B, but I'd like you to talk about it. Candidate B, you just listen. I'll give you your photograph in a moment.
>
> Candidate A, please tell us what you can see in your photograph.

(Candidate A) *Approximately one minute*

If there is a need to intervene, prompts rather than direct questions should be used.

Ask Candidate A to close his/her book.

Examiner

> Now, Candidate B, here is your photograph. It also shows people relaxing at home. *(Ask Candidate B to look at photo 2C on page II of the Student's Book.)* Please show it to Candidate A and tell us what you can see in the photograph.

(Candidate B) *Approximately one minute*

Ask the candidates to close their books before moving to Part 4.

Part 4 (3 minutes)

Tasks   Talking about one's likes and dislikes; expressing opinions: talking about habits.

Examiner   *Say to both candidates*:

> Your photographs showed people relaxing at home. Now, I'd like you to talk together about the things you do to relax at home, when you are alone and when you are with other people.

Allow the candidates enough time to complete the task without intervention.
Prompt only if necessary.

Back-up prompts
1. Talk about the things **you** do to relax at home.
2. Talk about relaxing **alone** or with other people.
3. Talk about **how** you would relax if you had more time / money.
4. Talk about **why** it is important to relax.

Thank you. That's the end of the test.

TEST 3

Part 1 (2–3 minutes)

Tasks   Identifying oneself; giving information about oneself; talking about interests.

Phase 1
Examiner

A/B   Good morning / afternoon / evening.
Can I have your mark sheets, please?

A/B   I'm ……….. and this is ………… .
He / she is just going to listen to us.

A   Now, what's your name?
Thank you.

B   And what's your name?
Thank you.

Back-up prompts

B   Candidate B, what's your surname?
How do you spell it?

Thank you.

| How do you write your family / second name? |

A   And, Candidate A, what's your surname?
How do you spell it?

Thank you.

| How do you write your family / second name? |

(Ask the following questions. Use candidates' names throughout. Ask Candidate A first.)

Where do you live / come from?

<u>Adult students</u>
Do you work or are you a student in . . .?
What do you do / study?

<u>School-age students</u>
Do you study English at school?
Do you like it?

Thank you.

(Repeat for Candidate B.)

Do you live in . . .?

Have you got a job?
What job do you do? / What subject(s) do you study?

Do you have English lessons?

Phase 2
Examiner

(Select one or more questions from the list to ask each candidate. Ask Candidate B first.)

	Back-up prompts
Do you enjoy studying English? Why (not)?	Do you like studying English?
Do you think that English will be useful for you in the future?	Will you use English in the future?
What did you do yesterday evening / last weekend?	Did you do anything yesterday evening / last weekend? What?
What do you enjoy doing in your free time?	What do you like to do in your free time?

Thank you.

(Introduction to Part 2)

In the next part, you are going to talk to each other.

Part 2 (2–3 minutes)

MAGAZINES FOR THE LIBRARY

Tasks   Discussing alternatives; expressing opinions; making choices.

Examiner   *Say to both candidates:*

> I'm going to describe a situation to you.
>
> A college wants to put some magazines in the library for the students.
> Talk together about the different magazines the college could put in the library, and say which would be most popular with the students.
>
> Here is a picture with some ideas to help you.

Ask both candidates to look at picture 3A on page V of the Student's Book and repeat the frame.

> I'll say that again.
>
> A college wants to put some magazines in the library for the students.
> Talk together about the different magazines the college could put in the library, and say which would be most popular with the students.
>
> All right? Talk together.

Allow the candidates enough time to complete the task without intervention. Prompt only if necessary.

Part 3 (3 minutes)

BUSY PEOPLE

Tasks   Describing people and places; saying where people and things are and what different people are doing.

Examiner   *Say to both candidates*:

> Now, I'd like each of you to talk on your own about something. I'm going to give each of you a photograph of busy people.
>
> Candidate A, here is your photograph. *(Ask Candidate A to look at photo 3B on page VI of the Student's Book.)* Please show it to Candidate B, but I'd like you to talk about it. Candidate B, you just listen. I'll give you your photograph in a moment.
>
> Candidate A, please tell us what you can see in the photograph.

(Candidate A)   *Approximately one minute*

If there is a need to intervene, prompts rather than direct questions should be used.

Ask Candidate A to close his/her book.

Examiner
> Now, Candidate B, here is your photograph. It also shows a busy person. *(Ask Candidate B to look at photo 3C on page VIII of the Student's Book.)* Please show it to Candidate A and tell us what you can see in the photograph.

(Candidate B)   *Approximately one minute*

Ask the candidates to close their books before moving to Part 4.

Part 4 (3 minutes)

Tasks   Talking about one's likes and dislikes; expressing opinions; talking about habits.

Examiner   *Say to both candidates*:

> Your photographs showed busy people. Now, I'd like you to talk together about times when you are busy and say if you enjoy being busy.

Allow the candidates enough time to complete the task without intervention. Prompt only if necessary.

Back-up prompts
1. Talk about times when **you** are busy.
2. Say how much you **enjoy** being busy.
3. Talk about the **busiest time** of your day / week / year.
4. Say why you **(dis)like** being busy.

Thank you. That's the end of the test.

TEST 4

Part 1 (2–3 minutes)

Tasks Identifying oneself; giving information about oneself; talking about interests.

Phase 1
Examiner

A/B Good morning / afternoon / evening.
Can I have your mark sheets, please?

A/B I'm ………… and this is ………… .
He / she is just going to listen to us.

A Now, what's your name?
Thank you.

B And what's your name?
Thank you.

Back-up prompts

B

| Candidate B, what's your surname? How do you spell it? Thank you. | How do you write your family / second name? |

A

| And, Candidate A, what's your surname? How do you spell it? Thank you. | How do you write your family / second name? |

| *(Ask the following questions. Use candidates' names throughout. Ask Candidate A first.)* Where do you live / come from? *Adult students* Do you work or are you a student in . . .? What do you do / study? *School-age students* Do you study English at school? Do you like it? Thank you. *(Repeat for Candidate B.)* | Do you live in . . .? Have you got a job? What job do you do? / What subject(s) do you study? Do you have English lessons? |

Phase 2
Examiner
(Select one or more questions from the list to ask each candidate. Ask Candidate B first.)

	Back-up prompts
Do you enjoy studying English? Why (not)?	Do you like studying English?
Do you think that English will be useful for you in the future?	Will you use English in the future?
What did you do yesterday evening / last weekend?	Did you do anything yesterday evening / last weekend? What?
What do you enjoy doing in your free time?	What do you like to do in your free time?

Thank you.

(Introduction to Part 2)

In the next part, you are going to talk to each other.

Part 2 (2–3 minutes)

TWINS

Tasks   Discussing alternatives; expressing opinions; making choices.

Examiner   *Say to both candidates:*

> I'm going to describe a situation to you.
>
> A young couple has just had twin baby boys and you would like to buy them a present. Talk together about the different things you could buy and then say which would be best.
>
> Here is a picture with some ideas to help you.

Ask both candidates to look at picture 4A on page VII of the Student's Book and repeat the frame.

> I'll say that again.
>
> A young couple has just had twin baby boys and you would like to buy them a present. Talk together about the different things you could buy and then say which would be best.
>
> All right? Talk together.

Allow the candidates enough time to complete the task without intervention. Prompt only if necessary.

Part 3 (3 minutes)

STUDENTS RELAXING

Tasks   Describing people and places; saying where people and things are and what different people are doing.

Examiner   *Say to both candidates*:

> Now, I'd like each of you to talk on your own about something. I'm going to give each of you a photograph of students relaxing.
>
> Candidate A, here is your photograph. *(Ask Candidate A to look at photo 4B on page VIII of the Student's Book.)* Please show it to Candidate B, but I'd like you to talk about it. Candidate B, you just listen. I'll give you your photograph in a moment.
>
> Candidate A, please tell us what you can see in the photograph.

(Candidate A) *Approximately one minute*

If there is a need to intervene, prompts rather than direct questions should be used.

Ask Candidate A to close his/her book.

Examiner   > Now, Candidate B, here is your photograph. It also shows students relaxing. *(Ask Candidate B to look at photo 4C on page VI of the Student's Book.)* Please show it to Candidate A and tell us what you can see in the photograph.

(Candidate B) *Approximately one minute*

Ask the candidates to close their books before moving to Part 4.

Part 4 (3 minutes)

Tasks   Talking about one's likes and dislikes; expressing opinions: talking about habits.

Examiner   *Say to both candidates*:

> Your photographs showed students relaxing. Now, I'd like you to talk together about where you go to relax and things you like to do there.

Allow the candidates enough time to complete the task without intervention. Prompt only if necessary.

> Thank you. That's the end of the test.

Back-up prompts
1. Talk about **where** you go to relax.
2. Talk about what you **do** to relax.
3. Talk about **when** you like to relax.
4. Talk about **why** it is important for students to relax.

Key

Test 1

READING

Part 1

1 C   2 B   3 A   4 A   5 B

Part 2

6 D   7 F   8 C   9 A   10 H

Part 3

11 A	12 A	13 A	14 B	15 B	16 B	17 A	18 A
19 B	20 B						

Part 4

21 C   22 D   23 A   24 B   25 D

Part 5

26 D	27 C	28 C	29 C	30 B	31 A	32 B	33 C
34 D	35 A						

WRITING

Part 1

1 (first) saw/had seen
2 has/has got
3 as/so difficult/hard
4 called
5 gives

Part 2

Task-specific Mark Scheme

The content elements that need to be covered are:

i   expression of thanks to candidate's friends
ii indication of what candidate enjoyed most about weekend
iii invitation for friends to stay with candidate

The following sample answers can be used as a guide when marking.

SAMPLE A (Test 1, Question 6: Letter to friends)

> Dear Tom and Kate
> I'm writting to say thankyou for the weekend. It was realy nice
> to go in Spain. I enjoyed most visit we did to arts museum. I
> want that you come and stay with me in summer.

Examiner Comments

All the elements are covered and the message is successfully communicated on the whole.

Mark: 4

SAMPLE B (Test 1, Question 6: Letter to friends)

> Dear friends
> Thanks you for nice weekend at yours house. I enjoyed
> most going to beach and play volley, and will remember the
> nice meal we eat in restraunt on Saturday. You will stay
> here soon.

Examiner Comments

The third element has not been successfully achieved, but the other two are sufficiently clear.

Mark: 3

SAMPLE C (Test 1, Question 6: Letter to friends)

> Hi guys!
> I write to thank you for a brilliant time last weekend. The computer game is the best – I am happy to be champion of the weekend! Come to my house next time for a new contest.
> Philip

Examiner Comments

All the elements are covered and the message is clearly communicated.

Mark: 5

SAMPLE D (Test 1, Question 7: Letter to a friend)

> Dear Erin,
> How are you? In your letter you told me you enjoyed a programme about dolphins on television, I don't really enjoy animal programmes as much. I don't watch television very often, I am more likely to watch films. But anyway I enjoyed ugly Betty the other day, I thougth it was really funny. Have you ever watched ugly Betty? I also enjoy watching the news sometimes.
> Probably the programme that I most watch is MTV, do you like MTV? I think is great but sometimes the music they choose is a bit strange.
> How often do you watch television?
> Lots of love. xx Bocia

Examiner Comments

This is a very good attempt. It is confident and natural, e.g. 'Have you ever watched Ugly Betty?', and 'How often do you watch television?'. There is a wide range of structures, e.g. 'I am more likely to watch films', 'Probably the programme that I most watch . . .'. It is also well organised with use of simple linking devices, e.g. 'but', 'but sometimes'. There are minor non-impeding errors, e.g. 'I think is great', and 'thougth'. No effort is required from the reader.

Band: 5

SAMPLE E (Test 1, Question 7: Letter to a friend)

Dear Sir,

I am writeing the letter intuldes my self my name is Ali Alhebsi I am

writing about Penfriend the television should be have because the

important I can watch anythik and I can watch the world and BBC and I

am enjoyed when I watch television and I've just seen a brilliant on

television I have enjoyed recently I watch television evryday two hours

For one dey but I watch lot of when I have weekends

I would appantion this accpeton this matter

your fiathfully,

Seed

Examiner Comments

This is a rather poor attempt. It shows a severely restricted command of language, e.g. 'I am writeing the letter intuldes my self . . .'. There is an inadequate range of structures and the absence of punctuation leads to serious incoherence, e.g. 'Should be have because the important I can watch anythik . . .'. Control is very poor at times and quite difficult to understand, e.g. 'I would appantion this accpeton this matter'. Requires excessive effort by the reader.

Band: 1

SAMPLE F (Test 1, Question 7: Letter to a friend)

Dear John,

How are you? I am very poor in this few weeks because I broke my leg when I was playing volleyball. I just stay at home and watch a lot of TV programmes in this week.

I watched an excellent programme called Alan Sugar. It is a competition which is a group of smart business men use different ideas to sell their products and try to make great profits in it. The winner can get a great job in Alan Sugar's Company. You can see how clever they are. I know you are interested in Business Study that's why I strongly recommend to you. It is on every Monday at 9:15pm in Channel 4.

How about your dolphins programme? It seems quite funny. Can you tell me more information about this programme?

Loves,

Jan

Examiner Comments

This is a good attempt. There is a more than adequate range of structures and vocabulary and fairly ambitious language, e.g. '. . . a group of smart business men use different ideas to sell their products and try to make great profits . . .', 'You can see how clever they are'. Organised through paragraphing and appropriate linking, e.g. '. . . because I broke my leg when I was playing . . .', '. . . that's why I strongly recommend . . .'. There are some non-impeding errors, e.g. 'I am very poor in this few weeks . . .', 'It is a competition which is a group . . .'. Requires only a little effort from the reader.

Band: 4

SAMPLE G **(Test 1, Question 8: Story)**

> I think about manything while I'm walking in the rain.
>
> To tell the true, I don't like rain. walking in the rain, too. But It remind me what I did at past. And it makes me to think about furthur. The sound of rain help me to calm down. I just like to think about myself while walking in the rain. Sometimes it makes me to be amuse by many sound. It is OK, I enjoy it, too.
>
> It gives me an exstra time what I couldn't have enough it in normal life.
>
> I like walking in the rain, except to what my shoes are wet To tell the true. The real reason why I don't like walking in the rain is that I have to what my shoes are wet.

Examiner Comments

This is an adequate attempt on the whole. The language is ambitious but flawed, e.g. 'It gives me an exsta time what I couldn't have enough it in normal life'. There is an adequate range but marred by errors, e.g. 'And it makes me to think about futhur'. There is some attempt at organisation, with some repetitive linking, e.g. 'to tell the true . . .', 'Sometimes . . .'. There are numerous errors, some of which are potentially impeding, e.g. 'Sometimes it make me to be amuse by many sound'. It requires some effort from the reader.

Band: 3

SAMPLE H (Test 1, Question 8: Story)

> I'll tell you story when, I walked in the rain. It was in the spring. I was in the park. It park has a lot of trees. When is weather is nice, and it raining, and you can hear birds are singing. I love rain. And also I like cickling? in the rain.

Examiner Comments

This is an inadequate attempt. The language is generally simplistic with a limited range of structures and vocabulary, e.g. 'I walked in the rain', 'I love rain', 'I was in the park'. Where there is more ambition this leads to inaccuracy, e.g. 'When is weather is nice . . . birds are singing'. There is some attempt at organisation with simple linking, e.g. 'and', 'when'. There are a number of errors, one of which is impeding: 'cickling'. It requires some effort from the reader. At fifty-four words this script can only obtain a maximum of 2.3. If this were full length, the script might achieve a slightly higher mark.

Band: 2

SAMPLE I (Test 1, Question 8: Story)

> Together walking in the rain, Jane and I sing cheerfully as usual. I turn my ipod on and skip between the trees.
>
> Suddenly, I find myself surrounded by some giant trees. I stop and scan around. A drop of rain drips onto my head.
>
> There she is! A purple spot shines in the darkness.
>
> 'Jane! Where were you? I was so scared! Come here, I have an umbrella. Come on.'
>
> She doesn't seem to have moved an inch.
>
> Now another man appears next to her. He is holding a soaked tenner while my sister drops the bag of white powder onto the wet, muddy ground.
>
> I start running towards her but wait – I cannot move.
>
> A hand as heavy as steel has already reached my shoulder.
>
> She stares at me in the most horrified way I have ever seen.

Examiner Comments

This is a very good attempt, above what is expected at PET level. The language is at times very ambitious, e.g. 'He is holding a soaked tenner', 'A hand as heavy as steel . . .'. There is a very wide range of structures and vocabulary. The narrative is well organized and extremely accurate. There is also good use of the narrative present tense and direct speech. No effort is required from the reader.

Band: 5

PAPER 2   LISTENING

Part 1

1 A   2 A   3 C   4 B   5 A   6 B   7 A

Part 2

8 A   9 C   10 C   11 A   12 A   13 B

Part 3

14   T/tiger(s)
15   A/aug(ust) (evenings)
16   1765
17   K/kitchen(s)
18   (old) F/fishing
19   S/sweet(s)(es)(ies) C/candy(s)/C/candies

Part 4

20 B   21 B   22 A   23 B   24 A   25 B

Key

Test 1 transcript

This is the Cambridge Preliminary English Test, Test 1.

There are four parts to the test. You will hear each part twice. For each part of the test there will be time for you to look through the questions and time for you to check your answers.

Write your answers on the question paper. You will have six minutes at the end of the test to copy your answers onto the answer sheet.

The recording will now be stopped.

Please ask any questions now, because you must not speak during the test.

[Pause]

Now open your question paper and look at Part 1.

PART 1   *There are seven questions in this part. For each question there are three pictures and a short recording. Choose the correct picture and put a tick in the box below it.*

Before we start, here is an example.

Where is the girl's hat?

Mum: Where's your new hat, Sally? I hope you haven't left it on the school bus.

Sally: Don't worry, Mum. I put it in my school bag because I was too hot.

Mum: Are you sure? I can't see it there. You probably dropped it in the road somewhere.

Sally: Oh, here it is – hanging in the hall. I forgot to take it this morning.

[Pause]

The first picture is correct so there is a tick in box A.

Look at the three pictures for Question 1 now.

[Pause]

Now we are ready to start. Listen carefully. You will hear each recording twice.

One. Where will the friends meet?

Girl: Hi, it's Maria. Got your message. Yeah, I'd like to go to the movies. There's a film called *Lightworld Two*, or a comedy – I don't mind which . . . Shall we meet outside the cinema?

Boy: Or, I know, at the coffee bar on the corner, we could have a snack before we go in. We could meet at the bus stop.

Girl: Mum's driving me into town this afternoon, to buy some trainers, so I won't have to get the bus. But something to eat first is a good idea. Shall we say six o'clock?

Boy: OK.

[Pause]

Now listen again.

[The recording is repeated]

[Pause]

Two. What has the girl forgotten to bring?

Boy: Drink up your coffee – we'll be late for class. What are you looking for now? Don't tell me you've left your essay at home. You said you were working on it till midnight.

Girl: Don't worry, it was the first thing I put in my bag – look, here it is. I won't be a second . . . just checking everything. Pen . . . now where did I . . .? Oh dear, you'll be able to lend me one, won't you? Keys? – oh, here they are, in my pocket as usual . . .

[Pause]

Now listen again.

[The recording is repeated]

[Pause]

Three. Which TV programme is on at nine o'clock tonight?

Woman: Because of the ski jumping finals we're late finishing, so there are some changes to this evening's programmes. We won't now show the *Nature Programme*, about the dolphins found near the Florida coast, at nine o'clock. Instead, Tim Wong's *Chinese Kitchen* will be at this time, an hour later than advertised. You can see the *Nature Programme* at its usual time next week.

[Pause]

Now listen again.

[The recording is repeated]

[Pause]

Four. How will the man book tickets for the show?

Woman: Shall we go to the Boat Show? It's on for three weeks – but you need to book if you want to go on the first night because there's a party.

Man: Really? Let's go. How do you book?

Woman: On the Internet or by phone . . . or there's a form to fill in, in this week's TV magazine with a discount on each ticket.

Man: I like saving money, but the post's always so slow. I prefer to talk to someone when I'm making a booking – just leave it to me.

[Pause]

Now listen again.

[The recording is repeated]

[Pause]

Five. What will the man do this winter?

Woman: Will you go on working as a gardener when winter comes, Jim? You'll get very cold and wet working outside.

Man: Well, last winter I took a job in a supermarket. They're advertising for staff again at the moment, but I prefer being in the fresh air – even when the weather's bad. I'd really like to get a job abroad in the sun, but all the ones I've seen need building skills, which I haven't got. So I'll just stay in my present job for the time being.

[Pause]

Now listen again.

[The recording is repeated]

[Pause]

Six. How does the man want the woman to help him?

Man: Sarah, could you do something for me?

Woman: Well, it depends what it is.

Man: I want to clean the bedroom windows this afternoon, but I lent the ladder to John . . . could you give me a lift to his house and then bring me back with the ladder?

Woman: Of course – no problem.

[Pause]

Now listen again.

[The recording is repeated]

[Pause]

Seven. Which house did the woman stay in?

Woman 1:   I love these photos of your holiday. Is this the house you stayed in? I love the balconies and all those plants growing up the walls. Oh, and there's a lovely big swimming pool.

Woman 2:   Let me see. Oh, you're looking at the wrong photo – that was the house our friends stayed in. Ours was exactly like that one, but we only had the sea to swim in. Here, let me show you a photo of our house. It was just as nice.

[Pause]

Now listen again.

[The recording is repeated]

[Pause]

That is the end of Part 1.

[Pause]

Now turn to Part 2, questions 8–13.

PART 2   *You will hear a news reporter called Angela Bond, talking on the radio about her job.*

For each question, put a tick in the correct box. You now have forty-five seconds to look at the questions for Part 2.

[Pause]

Now we are ready to start. Listen carefully. You will hear the recording twice.

Interviewer: And today in the studio we have a familiar face on television, Angela Bond, the news reporter. Angela, your job has taken you all over the world, hasn't it?

Angela: Yes. I've reported from a number of countries in Asia and I've just returned from the United States. I must say, it's good to be able to unpack my suitcase now that the job has brought me to Britain for at least six months.

Interviewer: Is the travelling what you enjoy about the job?

Angela: It's certainly interesting, but it can be annoying never knowing where I'm going to be next week! For me, the really exciting thing is being somewhere when a big news story is taking place and seeing it develop. Sometimes that can be quite dangerous, but all jobs have their disadvantages! And travelling gives me the chance to collect souvenirs.

Interviewer: What kind of things?

Angela: Mostly things for my flat. I'm mad about anything Chinese and so when I was in Hong Kong, I got a really nice table and some chairs – and in Turkey I spend a lot of money on carpets. Then I've got pictures and other bits of art from Thailand and India. The flat's getting a bit crowded!

Interviewer: It sounds colourful! Do you have a regular working day?

Angela: Not really. At the moment I'm one of the team that reads the evening news, so sometimes I'm on at six thirty, and sometimes at ten o'clock. But that's at the end of the day. It all starts in the morning at eight thirty when I phone the office to see what has happened and what they want me to go and report on.

Interviewer: So you don't have much time for a social life?

Angela: It's better now I'm in London and can see my boyfriend more often. My sister introduced us. He came round for dinner when I was staying with her a year ago. We have a lot in common. He's a lawyer and I studied law at university. Also we've found that we lived in Hong Kong at the same time, although we never met.

Interviewer: What do you like to do in your free time?

Angela: Well, cooking is something new I'm trying because I can't do it when I'm travelling. But I'm not very good at it yet so I find it a bit stressful. One of the best things I've bought recently was a boat and when I want to feel calm and peaceful I go for a sail on the river. It never fails!

Interviewer: Angela – thanks.

[Pause]

Now listen again.

[The recording is repeated]

[Pause]

That is the end of Part 2.

[Pause]

Now turn to Part 3, questions 14–19.

PART 3 *You will hear a radio programme about some historic places to visit.*

For each question, fill in the missing information in the numbered space. You now have twenty seconds to look at Part 3.

[Pause]

Now we are ready to start. Listen carefully. You will hear the recording twice.

Man: Are you interested in history? Well, I'd like to tell you about some of the historic places open to visitors in this part of the country.

Let's start with the oldest first. *Black Rock Caves* have been here for over two million years. And, for half a million years, they were home to people and various animals, particularly tigers. You can explore these ancient homes and imagine what life was like for the people who lived there. The caves are open daily from April to October. A special attraction on evenings in August is a walk by candlelight. Don't take this tour if you are afraid of the dark!

Next I recommend a visit to *Salter House*. This was built by Sir Joshua Salter and dates back to seventeen sixty-five. The Salter family are still living there today. The house became famous in nineteen eighty-two when the television series *Aunt Dorothy* was filmed there. The furniture and paintings are well worth seeing, but the attraction nobody wants to miss is the kitchen. This is where Aunt Dorothy cooked her enormous meals and gave advice to anyone who passed through this part of the house.

And don't forget to visit *The Old Port*. You will need several hours to see everything there, especially if you take a trip along the riverside in an old tram as far as the fishing village. The guides there all wear traditional costume and you too get the chance to try on clothes from a hundred years ago. You can buy gifts in the old village stores and eat delicious snacks in the Tea Shop. If you visit the village factory, you can see how sweets were made a hundred years ago, and taste them, too.

So, you see there's plenty of . . .

[Pause]

Now listen again.

[The recording is repeated]

[Pause]

That is the end of Part 3.

[Pause]

Now turn to Part 4, questions 20–25.

Key

PART 4   *Look at the six sentences for this part. You will hear a conversation between a boy, Marcus, and a girl, Catherine, about their homework.*

Decide if each sentence is correct or incorrect. If it is correct, put a tick in the box under A for YES. If it is not correct, put a tick in the box under B for NO. You now have twenty seconds to look at the questions for Part 4.

[Pause]

Now we are ready to start. Listen carefully. You will hear the recording twice.

Marcus: I feel awful. I've got two lots of homework to do today, and all I want to do after school is relax. It's not fair.

Catherine: Of course you've got a lot. You didn't do any yesterday, did you?

Marcus: No, I didn't. I had football practice, and after that I was just too tired for anything else.

Catherine: Well, maybe you could do more homework at the weekends, so you have time for football and other things during the week.

Marcus: But at the weekend I often go out with my family. On Sunday we went to the Science Museum. It was great. I wouldn't want to miss doing things like that just because I've got homework!

Catherine: Actually, you're quite lucky. I never do anything like that. Homework isn't everything . . . I'm sure you learnt just as much there.

Marcus: Yes, but I don't suppose the teachers will be interested in that . . . I've got today's maths to do, and I expect it'll take me hours.

Catherine: I tell you what . . . you can come round to my house this afternoon and we'll work on it together.

Marcus: I don't know . . . You're really good at maths. You'll just finish it quickly and I can't do that.

Catherine: It's not a competition, is it? It's more important that we both finish it, and working together'll be much more fun.

Marcus: But if I don't do it by myself, I could be in trouble with the teacher.

Catherine: Well, we'll tell her you're finding it difficult and so I'm going to try and help you understand it. I'm sure she won't mind that.

Marcus: Alright then, thank you. Perhaps I'll feel better about maths if you help me. At the moment, I still don't know where to begin.

Catherine: Don't worry, we'll get there.

[Pause]

Now listen again.

[The recording is repeated]

[Pause]

That is the end of Part 4.

[Pause]

You now have six minutes to check and copy your answers on to the answer sheet.

Note: Teacher, stop the recording here and time six minutes. Remind students when there is **one** minute remaining.

That is the end of the test.

Test 2

PAPER 1   READING AND WRITING

READING

Part 1

1 B   2 C   3 C   4 A   5 B

Part 2

6 F   7 H   8 E   9 G   10 C

Part 3

11 B   12 A   13 A   14 B   15 A   16 B   17 B   18 A   19 B
20 B

Part 4

21 C   22 A   23 D   24 D   25 B

Part 5

26 B   27 C   28 D   29 B   30 C   31 B   32 D   33 A   34 D
35 B

WRITING

Part 1

1 have not/haven't/(I)'ve not
2 (very/too/that/so) far (away) from
3 unless/except if/until/till/before
4 don't you/not
5 (really/much/far/unfortunately) too

Part 2

Task-specific Mark Scheme
The content elements that need to be covered are:

i   reason why candidate's school was chosen
ii indication of who or what was filmed
iii mention of when programme can be seen on TV

The following sample answers can be used as a guide when marking.

SAMPLE A **(Test 2, Question 6: Email to Alice)**

> Dear Alice:
> Hey Alice, how're you. I hope you're healthy.
> Yesterday I was sitting in the school yard, when a man came in and was talking to the Headmaster telling him about the Matrix movie they were going to film.
> The premier is on Saturday. Bye
> Patricio

Examiner Comments

Points 1 and 2 are missing. Point 3 relates to a cinema premiere.

Mark: 1

SAMPLE B **(Test 2, Question 6: Email to Alice)**

> Dear Alice,
> Yesterday a TV company came to my school to film a terror film. They chose my school because it's very old and big. This film is going to be on TV next wednesday because they have to film more yet.
> Best wishes,
> Jose

Examiner Comments

Points 1 and 3 are clear. However, point 2 has not been addressed.

Mark: 3

SAMPLE C (Test 2, Question 6: Email to Alice)

> Dear Alice:
> Yesterday a TV company came to out school because our class won the competition of writting a story about a man lost in a mountain.
> They filmed us reading the story and they told us that the programme will be shown on channel five.
> Your Friend.

Examiner Comments

A good and clear response.

Mark: 5

SAMPLE D (Test 2, Question 7: Letter to a friend)

> Dear Anna,
> Hi, how are you doing?
> How is your family? Are they alright? Please say hello to them from me.
> In the letter you told about your holiday, didn't you? In, my opinion, if I were you, I'd go with my family. Because, you told me your parents were always busy so you couldn't talk with them often. Why don't you go with them? You can have a nice talking with your parents. Your parents must want to go with you. Next year is your last year of the university so you'll be much busier than now. Otherwise, you can't go to the trip with your family anymore, perhaps. Family time is precious, I think. So I'd recommend you to go with your family.
> Anyway, take care of your self.
> I hope I hear from you soon. xxx
> Love,
> Mayu

Examiner Comments

This is a very good attempt with confident and ambitious use of language, e.g. 'Next year is your last year of the university so you'll be much busier than now.' There is a wide range of structures and vocabulary, e.g. 'Family time is precious, I think'. It is well organised and coherent, with simple linking, e.g. 'In my opinion', 'Because,' 'Otherwise' and 'so'. Some minor non-impeding errors do exist, which are not always due to ambition, e.g. 'You can have a nice talking . . .' but no effort is required from the reader.

Band: 5

SAMPLE E (Test 2, Question 7: Letter to a friend)

Hi, Jenny.

Would you prefer go somewhere with you friends

Did you already choice the place where will you go your friends

If you don't choice somewhere yet, I think, what you go on holiday with your parents is better.

Because, whenever you can go somewhere with your friends but this chance that you have holiday with your parent will seldom come to you.

Besides, If you don't go with your parents, they will dissapoint and sad.

So, I recommend that you go this holiday with your parents

Love

JINA.

Examiner Comments

An adequate attempt that shows ambition but is flawed, e.g. 'If you don't go with your parents, they will dissapoint and sad.' There is an adequate range of structures, e.g. 'So, I recommend that you go . . .' and vocabulary, e.g. 'whenever', 'seldom'. Some attempt at organisation is evident, with linking devices, e.g. 'Besides', 'So', 'Because'. A number of non-impeding errors are present, e.g. 'Did you already choice the place where will you go your friends' and some effort is required from the reader.

Band: 3

SAMPLE F (Test 2, Question 7: Letter to a friend)

My parent want me to go on holiday with them this sumer but I would prefer to go somewhere with my friends. Then just because I a holiday per year my parents thoung It is very good idea they give money for going to the a beach and make big party; so I thoung fantastic idea of my parent: Then they explening me. We have all the year for stay together easter Christmas mothers day for my family IT's very important

So then I am so happy.

Examiner Comments

This is an inadequate attempt. The quality of language is limited with an inadequate range of structures and vocabulary, e.g. '. . . they give money for going to the a beach . . .'. The punctuation is erratic together with poor spelling and numerous structural errors leading to some incoherence, e.g. 'Then just because I a holiday per year my parents thoung . . .'. Considerable effort required on behalf of the reader.

Band: 2

SAMPLE G (Test 2, Question 8: As soon as I saw the handwriting . . .)

> As soon as I saw the handwriting on the envelope I smiled. I read the letter and it
> said i was invited to a chrismas ball – at 11:30pm.
> In the next evening I started to wonder what i will wear I went to my closet and
> searched for nice clothes but idin't find one then my friend came over with a bunch
> of clothes saying that is was for me so i took it and I started serching and
> searching until I found something it was a white top with a pink skirt. I looked
> fabulous in it. then the next minute i thougt I had nice high heeled white shoes but i
> dint have them I looked in my shoe rack and I found one for my sister and I wore
> it. the went to the ball and had so much fun

Examiner Comments

This is an adequate attempt. It is at times fairly ambitious, e.g. 'my friend came over with a bunch
of clothes', with a more than adequate range of structures and vocabulary, e.g. 'I started serching
and searching until I found something', 'high heeled white shoes'. Punctuation, however, is
erratic, frequently lacking full stops and commas, e.g. 'In the next evening . . . pink skirt'. Some
linking is evident, e.g. 'but', 'so'. There are a number of errors but mostly non-impeding, e.g. ' In
the next evening', 'that is was for me'. Some effort is required by the reader.

Band: 3

SAMPLE H (Test 2, Question 8: As soon as I saw the handwriting . . .)

> As soon as I saw the handwriting on the envelope, I smiled. That was it!! I waited
> this letter for three weeks now!
> I went to London for an audition at the Royal ballet school three weeks ago. This is
> one of the best dance schools in the world and I had a letter from the school
> director to know if I was accepted. I was shaking. I was scared . . . I get slowly
> the handwriting in the envelope and I opened my eyes. It said: "Dear Miss Boissiere,
> we are happy to tell you that you have got a place at the Royal ballet school in
> September . . ." I couldn't read anymore because of my tears. That was the best day
> of my life!

Examiner Comments

This is a very good attempt. There is confident and ambitious use of language, e.g. 'This is one of
the best dance schools in the world', and a wide range of structures and vocabulary, e.g. 'I went
to London for an audition', 'I couldn't read anymore because of my tears.' It is well organized and
coherent through narrative development. There are a few errors, including one that is potentially
impeding; 'I get slowly the handwriting . . .'. Generally, though, apart from this example, it
requires no effort from the reader.

Band: 5

SAMPLE I (Test 2, Question 8: As soon as I saw the handwriting . . .)

> As soon as I saw the handwriting on the envelope I smiled because I know who the sender is. It's been a long time since we talk so I was very happy to hear from her. She is my bestfriend. Her name is Parvin, she is a Mauritian. She's been on vacation for two months already. She's telling all the places she visited. She visited four countries. She was amazed of the people she meets, the kind of food they eat and the kind of dress they wear. One more thing she likes is that she can buy lots of things without spending too much. She wants me to be with her for the next trip.

Examiner Comments

A good attempt. There is fairly ambitious use of language, e.g. 'One more thing she likes . . . without spending too much', with a more than adequate range of structures and vocabulary, e.g. 'It's been a long time since we talk so I was very happy to hear from her.' There is evidence of organization through thematic linking, though little use is made of linking devices. Some errors exist but they are generally non-impeding, e.g. 'She's telling all the places she visited', 'She was amazed of the people she meets . . .'. Requires only a little effort on the part of the reader.

Band: 4

PAPER 2   LISTENING

Part 1

1 B   2 A   3 B   4 C   5 B   6 B   7 A

Part 2

8 A   9 A   10 C   11 B   12 B   13 A

Part 3

14   O/opera(s)
15   T/ten (students) /10
16   (to) R/relax
17   C/classic(al) (s) (songs)
18   (the) S/salad (s) (bar)
19   T/Tuesday T/tues

Part 4

20 B   21 A   22 B   23 A   24 B   25 B

Test 2 transcript

This is the Cambridge Preliminary English Test, Test 2.

There are four parts to the test. You will hear each part twice. For each part of the test there will be time for you to look through the questions and time for you to check your answers.

Write your answers on the question paper. You will have six minutes at the end of the test to copy your answers onto the answer sheet.

The recording will now be stopped.

Please ask any questions now, because you must not speak during the test.

[Pause]

Now open your question paper and look at Part 1.

PART 1   *There are seven questions in this part. For each question there are three pictures and a short recording. Choose the correct picture and put a tick in the box below it.*

Before we start, here is an example.

How many eggs do you need to make the cake?

Woman: That cake you made yesterday was lovely. Could you show me how to make one?

Man: Mmm . . . It's really simple. Have you got any butter?

Woman: Yes, I've got about a hundred grams.

Man: That's fine. And you'll need a hundred and fifty grams of flour and sugar. You mix the butter and sugar together, add one egg, mix some more, then add another one. After that you add some flour, stir well, then put in some more flour. Then you just pour it into a cake tin and bake it. Easy!

[Pause]

The first picture is correct so there is a tick in box A.

Look at the three pictures for Question 1 now.

[Pause]

Now we are ready to start. Listen carefully. You will hear each recording twice.

One. Where are the dictionaries?

Man: As this is your first visit to the library, I'll show you round. As you can see, shelves are clearly labelled according to subject. Most books you may take home with you but some, such as foreign language dictionaries, must stay in the library. These can be found over there behind the computers and it's best if you take them to the desks by the window and study them there. Or you can use these armchairs if you prefer to sit somewhere more comfortable.

[Pause]

Now listen again.

[The recording is repeated]

[Pause]

Two. Which evening dress does the woman decide to wear?

Man: Why are you taking so long to decide what to wear tomorrow night? The black dress with the long sleeves will be fine!

Woman: Mmm . . . Long sleeves are a bit uncomfortable, but yes, it's a nice dress. Trouble is, I've lent my short-sleeved dress to Angela. That would be perfect, it's a long dress with a wide belt . . . Anyway, let's see what I've got here . . . this one, also black, short-sleeved – but it's got white flowers on the sleeves.

Man: Why don't you phone Angela and get your dress back?

Woman: Yes, I think I will.

[Pause]

Now listen again.

[The recording is repeated]

[Pause]

Three. What is the man's job now?

Man: When I was young, I used to paint. I always dreamed of being an artist, painting pictures for a living. But I didn't do very well at school and so I left early to join my dad working in the family photography business. After a few years of that I got bored, and felt I wanted to go back and study. That's when I did my degree and teacher training, and I've taught photography ever since, although I still paint in my spare time.

[Pause]

Now listen again.

[The recording is repeated]

[Pause]

Four. Which calendar will the boy buy?

Boy: Mum asked me to buy her a calendar. Shall I get this one with pictures of mountains, or this one with boats on it?

Girl: She loves sailing, so get that one. I like that one with wild animals, but I don't suppose Mum would. And you can't get the one with mountains because she had that last year.

Boy: Yes, I know. I'll get the one you suggested then.

[Pause]

Now listen again.

[The recording is repeated]

[Pause]

Five. What time will the writer arrive at the bookshop?

Man: All fans of Peter Robbins should go to the South Street book store tomorrow afternoon, where Peter will sign copies of his book *Love of Life* and answer questions. He is expected at a quarter past two and promises to stay until half past three, when he has to leave for another appointment. Get there as soon as you can because, if it's anything like Peter's last visit, queues will start to form at quarter to two or even earlier. Don't miss this opportunity to meet everyone's favourite writer.

[Pause]

Now listen again.

[The recording is repeated]

[Pause]

Six. What did the woman leave in the restaurant?

Man: Hello . . . back again. Did you leave something behind?

Woman: Yes. I don't know if you remember but when I wanted to pay the bill I couldn't find my purse, so I emptied everything out of my bag to look for it, and that's when I took my keys out. When I got back to the car, I realised they weren't in my bag . . .

Man: Which table were you sitting at?

[Pause]

Now listen again.

[The recording is repeated]

[Pause]

Seven. Where is the bicycle?

Boy: I think someone's stolen my bicycle. I left it by that tree on the pavement, but it's not there any more.

Girl: Perhaps it got in my father's way when he was parking his car.

Boy: Oh yeah, I think you're right. It's on the other side of the road, by that street light. He probably moved it. I'll remember to leave it well away from the tree in future!

Girl: Yes, and lock it next time as well.

[Pause]

Now listen again.

[The recording is repeated]

[Pause]

That is the end of Part 1.

[Pause]

Now turn to Part 2, questions 8–13.

PART 2   *You will hear a radio interview with Jack Williams, who is talking about a town called Swanton. For each question, put a tick in the correct box. You now have forty-five seconds to look at the questions for Part 2.*

           [Pause]

           Now we are ready to start. Listen carefully. You will hear the recording twice.

Interviewer: Oh, what a wonderful view! I'm here with Jack Williams, who's telling me about his home town of Swanton.

Jack: Yes, the top of this hill is the best place to see the area. Swanton is on the coast – you can see the harbour from here – but in fact the town is built along the river Dean. This river comes from a lake in the mountains, over there in the distance, then flows down to the flat land below us where the town is built.

Interviewer: What do you most like about living here?

Jack: About Swanton? Oh, it's an important industrial town and a port, so there's lots of activity. And there's a forest behind the town with interesting wildlife. But the most exciting thing for me is the mountains. I go climbing whenever I get the chance.

Interviewer: What about entertainment?

Jack: There's plenty of entertainment. A big centre was built last year to encourage the arts – very modern. It's got a cinema, a theatre and an art gallery. And there's football. The local team hasn't done so well lately. A few years ago we nearly won the Cup. And our area is famous for music – not in Swanton itself, but there's a well-known music festival in the next town.

Interviewer: But there are problems with the environment.

Jack: We're working on that. The river was a great place for fish, but the water got so polluted by the factories that most of the fish disappeared. Well, we've cleaned the river up now, and the fish are starting to come back. But I'm unhappy about Swanton woods. The trees are quite healthy, but if you look, there are no birds there, and that's because pollution has reduced the number of insects.

Interviewer: Swanton's growing fast. Are you pleased about the way it's changed?

Jack: You've got to move with the times. It was completely different when I was a boy. In those days everybody worked in the factories, and the families all knew each other. Maybe it was a little boring. Today there are hundreds of different companies, and so many new houses that some people don't even know their neighbours. There are disadvantages, but it's impossible to be bored with all the things going on.

Interviewer: And what about Swanton's future?

Jack: Education is important to us. We have a fine university, which specialises in advanced technology. And a huge shopping centre, just built, which is bringing in double the number of visitors – good news for us. And last year we improved our airport, so more planes can come in.

[Pause]

Now listen again.

[The recording is repeated]

[Pause]

That is the end of Part 2.

[Pause]

Now turn to Part 3, questions 14–19.

PART 3   *You will hear a woman talking on the radio about a singing course she attended.*

For each question, fill in the missing information in the numbered space. You now have twenty seconds to look at Part 3.

[Pause]

Now we are ready to start. Listen carefully. You will hear the recording twice.

Interviewer: I've just come back from a short music course called *Singing for Beginners*. It was at Brownstoke College, which is just to the north of London.

A woman called Lena Phipps runs these three-day courses for people with no previous experience of singing. Lena used to be an opera singer, but no longer appears on the stage. Nowadays she occasionally sings in jazz clubs, but spends most of her time teaching. She was excellent!

There were only nine of us on the course I attended, five men and four women, and Lena never takes more than ten students on a course. This means that everyone has lots of attention and plenty of opportunity to sing.

We were all very nervous at the beginning, but every class begins with some exercises to help students relax. These are followed by warm-up exercises to improve the quality of the voice.

During the three days, students learn around twenty songs in a variety of different styles, depending on the interests of the class members. There are classical and modern songs, including pop songs. By the last day, everyone was confident enough to perform their favourite song on their own!

I would really recommend this course. Brownstoke College is an old building surrounded by a beautiful garden. Accommodation is very comfortable – the single and twin rooms are clean and warm, and three meals a day are included in the cost; a cooked breakfast, lunch and an evening meal. The lunch is very good, and the salads can be recommended.

Courses begin on the last Tuesday of the month, so the next one begins on the 24th of September and continues until Thursday the 26th of September. I would advise you to reserve a place early, because it's certain to be very popular!

[Pause]

Now listen again.

[The recording is repeated]

[Pause]

That is the end of Part 3.

[Pause]

Now turn to Part 4, questions 20–25.

Key

PART 4   *Look at the six sentences for this part. You will hear a conversation between a man, Marco, and his wife, Sarah, about a film they have just seen at the cinema.*

Decide if each sentence is correct or incorrect. If it is correct, put a tick in the box under A for YES. If it is not correct, put a tick in the box under B for NO.

You now have twenty seconds to look at the questions for Part 4.

[Pause]

Now we are ready to start. Listen carefully. You will hear the recording twice.

Marco: So . . . what did you think of the film?

Sarah: Mmm . . . I didn't know what it would be like. I wasn't very keen to see it when you suggested it, but I'm pleased I came now.

Marco: Oh, good. I'm glad you liked it.

Sarah: And it was great to see scenes of London in the background. I'm sure I recognised the hotel where we stayed last year.

Marco: Mmm . . . I wasn't sure it was London at first, but then I recognised the place we stayed, too. It was nice to see it, wasn't it?

Sarah: Oooh, my legs are stiff from sitting for so long. Over three hours, wasn't it?

Marco: At least. I didn't notice the time going by at all, though – I was interested in the film. I thought it was good – and I usually hate long films! I often find them a bit boring.

Sarah: Well, the man sitting next to me didn't find it as interesting as you did. Did you see he fell asleep after fifteen minutes?

Marco: Oh, I didn't notice.

Sarah: And the two women in front kept talking right through the exciting bits. I couldn't concentrate. I was really angry.

Marco: Mmm . . . it's a shame they talked when the main actor was on screen. I can't remember his name, but I liked his acting. He was brilliant.

Sarah: Mmm . . . you're right. He must be a new actor – I haven't seen him before. He's obviously going to have a great career.

Marco: Mmm . . . and the director's really good, too. I think I prefer the other films he's made, though. His earliest one was probably the most entertaining.

Sarah: Oh, I must see that, then. Perhaps we can get it on DVD . . .

Marco: Good idea. We could stop at the shop on the way home, and see if they've got it.

Sarah: Right.

[Pause]

Now listen again.

[The recording is repeated]

[Pause]

That is the end of Part 4.

[Pause]

You now have six minutes to check and copy your answers on to the answer sheet.

Note: Teacher, stop the recording here and time six minutes. Remind students when there is **one** minute remaining.

That is the end of the test.

Test 3

PAPER 1   READING AND WRITING

READING

Part 1

1 B   2 C   3 B   4 C   5 A

Part 2

6 F   7 A   8 G   9 D   10 B

Part 3

11 A   12 B   13 B   14 A   15 B   16 A   17 B   18 B   19 A
20 A

Part 4

21 D   22 B   23 A   24 B   25 C

Part 5

26 D   27 B   28 A   29 C   30 C   31 D   32 A   33 B   34 C
35 D

WRITING

Part 1

1   the most famous/the best known
2   (about) who
3   interested
4   painting/finishing/doing/working on/on
5   much (money)/many pounds/dollars/euros

Part 2

Task-specific Mark Scheme

The content elements that need to be covered are:

i   suggestion of a new time to meet on Tuesday
ii reason why candidate needs to change the time
iii reminder to friend of where to meet

The following sample answers can be used as a guide when marking.

SAMPLE A **(Test 3, Question 6: Email to Sally)**

Dear Shally
Hi you remmeber that we decided to meet next Tuesday at 7:00 pm but sorry I tell you due to my mother is coming from U.S.A. So, I have pick her at 2:00 Pm ON 7:00 Pm, so I would be come on the town street of café on Tuesday OK
I hope you understand Bye
Thankyou
Your's friend
(signature)

Examiner Comments

The message is only partly communicated to the reader due to an element of incoherence. The second content point is clear, but the first point is missing and the third point is somewhat vague.

Mark: 2

SAMPLE B **(Test 3, Question 6: Email to Sally)**

Dear Sally
How are you? I hope you are fine. As we decided to meet on Tuesday 12:00 a.m, but I have to change the time i.e 4:30 pm because my mum's relatives are coming early in the morning 8:00 o'clock. So, Mum need my help in cooking and serving food. She also want me to attend the guests nicely. So I need to change the time. OK, we will meet at our favourite Restaurant Royal's
Yours friend
(signature)

Examiner Comments

All three content elements are covered appropriately.

Mark: 5

SAMPLE C (Test 3, Question 6: Email to Sally)

> *Sara Can we change the time we had to meet each other on Tuesday? I must go out with my mother to buy Sofia's birthday present. Will we meet at the music shop as we arranged.*

Examiner Comments

The first content element is omitted but the other two are clearly communicated.

Mark: 3

SAMPLE D (Test 3, Question 7: Letter to a penfriend)

> *Dear Mike,*
>
> *Thanks you for write me. About your question I think that go to a large school in the centre of town could be better than the other option. In my opinion if the school is big has a lot of classes, different teachers, a big librery to study, a cafeteria to have a break . . . And probably a lots of public transport to be on time. Also It's depends your tarty, because some people preffer a small school because there are a few people and sometime is better than to be in a class with 30 classmate. So in the end is your choose. You have to know what is better to you.*
>
> *With love,*
>
> *Estefania*

Examiner Comments

This is an adequate attempt. The language is quite ambitious but is somewhat flawed in places, e.g. 'And probably a lots of public transport to be on time.' There is an adequate range of structures, e.g. 'a large school . . . could be better than the other option', plus relevant school vocabulary, e.g. 'classmates', 'librery', 'cafeteria'. There is some attempt at organisation. Sentences are linked with 'In my opinion', 'because', 'So in the end'. A number of errors are present but are mostly non-impeding except for 'It's depends your tarty'. Some effort is required by the reader.

Band: 3

SAMPLE E (Test 3, Question 7: Letter to a penfriend)

> My friend,
>
> Hi! How's life now a days? I just do hope that everything is doing well.
>
> It is really hard or you to choice on what school are you going to. Well my friend tell the truth to your parents that if you don't want a small school in the countryside and you prefer a larger school in the town center so that they will know what to do regarding your studies. If your place is very far from the town center maybe you can rent a small room near your school. But that still depends if your parents will agree with that suggestion, maybe if they don't you have to go home everyday as long as your schedule is not hectic.
>
> Till here, I mis you and regards to your parents.

Examiner Comments

This is a very good effort. It shows confident and ambitious use of language, e.g. 'so that they will know what to do regarding your studies', There is a wide range of structures, e.g. 'as long as your schedule is not hectic' and vocabulary, e.g. 'doing well', 'prefer a larger school', 'depends', 'suggestion'. It is well organized and paragraphed. Sentences are appropriately linked, e.g. 'well my friend', 'that still depends', 'if', 'so that'. What errors there are tend to be minor and non-impeding, e.g. 'till here', 'to choice on what school'. No effort required by the reader.

Band: 5

SAMPLE F (Test 3, Question 7: Letter to a penfriend)

> Dear Risa.
> Thanks for your letter.
> I heard you're moving with your family to a different area next month, and you are now considering about choosing between going to a small school in the country side or a large school in the centre of town I think both of them have advantages and disadvantages, but I suggest a small school in the country side. Because there are not too many people in school, you can be friend easily, I think. And I remember that you like countryside because there are close to nature and there are lots of fresh air and park. Of course, a large school also could be good. Because it's in the centre of town you can visit a lot of shops, museums, theatres or galleries.
> I'm looking for your letter,
> See you

Examiner Comments

A good attempt. The use of language is fairly ambitious, e.g. 'I heard you're moving', 'both of them have advantages and disadvantages', and there is a more than adequate range of structures, e.g. 'I suggest a small school', 'I remember that you like', and vocabulary, e.g. 'museums, theatres or galleries'. There is evidence of organization with paragraphing and some linking of sentences, e.g. 'Of course', 'and', 'but', 'because'. There are some errors, generally non-impeding, e.g. 'I'm looking for your letter', 'considering about choosing', 'you can be friend easily'. Only a little effort required by the reader.

Band: 4

SAMPLE G (Test 3, Question 8: Phone still on the table)

> As the man left the café, Maria saw that his phone was still on the table. in this café was only three table one of Rose the man on the other is Mario and me He thdred was two far from us in the corner when this man let Maria notice that he sorget his phone she tell me and I said for her wow it's nice phone let bring it she said at first no, than why not. I look around me than I took the phone we start search we found that the man is photography and he come for a job in this country and later the phone is rang me afraid to answer in the beginning than I said may be this man he search for his phone lets answer and return the phone for her. when we answer the man said can I speak to the lady pleas he was in love with her.

Examiner Comments

This is an inadequate attempt. Some range and ambition are attempted, but are usually unsuccessful and seriously flawed. There is some attempt at linking, e.g. 'when . . .', 'at first . . .', but errors in the structure and punctuation lead to incoherence. There are numerous errors which sometimes impede communication, e.g. 'I said for her wow', 'we start search', 'the phone is rang me afraid to answer . . .'. It requires considerable effort on the part of the reader.

Band: 2

Key

SAMPLE H **(Test 3, Question 8: Phone still on the table)**

As the man left the café. Maria saw that his phone was still on the table I was drinking a coffee with my friend after a second I saw a phone on the table so I called waitress and said about this problem. She said that she had known him many years and she took the mobile phone and went. After one week I went to café again and I saw the man. He was calling and I went to him and I said hello, I'm Maria. He turned back and saw me. I said, thanks a lot. After that time, I met him in the cafe and we became friends.

Examiner Comments

This is a good attempt. There is fairly ambitious use of language, including examples of indirect speech, e.g. 'She said that she had known him many years . . .'. There is also a more than adequate range of structures and vocabulary, e.g. 'I was drinking a coffee', 'He turned back and saw me', '. . . and we became friends'. The story is organised chronologically into paragraphs, with appropriate linking, e.g. 'After one week', 'so', 'After that time'. Some errors exist but are generally non-impeding, e.g. '. . . so I called waitress and said about this problem'. Only a little effort is required of the reader. After the prompt sentence, Maria becomes 'I'. However, this is consistent and is not penalised.

Band: 4

SAMPLE I (Test 3, Question 8: Phone still on the table)

As the man left the café, Maria saw that his phone was still on the table then she stood up and went to take it, after taking it she ran towards the man and stopped him to give him his phone. The man checked his pockets to make sure that it was its, his pockets were empty and he took the phone by thanking her and began to chat with her. He gave her his phone's number and took hers as well, they arranged one day to meet again although they were calling each other from time to time saying nothing important, the day which they'd arranged arrived and both of them were there on time. They had a good time and finishing by falling in love.

Examiner Comments

This is a very good attempt. It shows confident and ambitious use of language, e.g. 'The man checked his pockets to make sure'. There is a wide range of structures, e.g. 'the day which they'd arranged arrived' and vocabulary, e.g. 'both of them', 'his pockets were empty'. The narrative is coherent with simple linking, using 'which', 'then', 'after', 'as well'. Errors are minor and non-impeding, e.g. 'to make sure that it was its', 'He gave her his phone's number'. It requires no effort from the reader.

Band: 5

PAPER 2   LISTENING

Part 1

1 B   2 C   3 C   4 A   5 C   6 B   7 C

Part 2

8 B   9 C   10 A   11 C   12 A   13 B

Part 3

14 (of) M/march
    (of) M/mar
15 520
16 (by) (the) T/train(s)
    (by) R/rail (way/road)
17 (an/your/their) I/identity/ID(-) C/card(s)
18 BIRINFO/birinfo/BIR INFO/ bir info
19 (on/this) F/Friday/F/fri

Part 4

20 A   21 B   22 B   23 A   24 B   25 B

Test 3 transcript

This is the Cambridge Preliminary English Test, Test 3.

There are four parts to the test. You will hear each part twice. For each part of the test there will be time for you to look through the questions and time for you to check your answers.

Write your answers on the question paper. You will have six minutes at the end of the test to copy your answers onto the answer sheet.

The recording will now be stopped.

Please ask any questions now, because you must not speak during the test.

[Pause]

Now open your question paper and look at Part 1.

PART 1   *There are seven questions in this part. For each question there are three pictures and a short recording. Choose the correct picture and put a tick in the box below it.*

Before we start, here is an example.

How did the woman get to work?

Woman: Oh, I'm so sorry I'm late – I missed the bus. I was trying to decide whether to walk or go back and get my bike when I saw my neighbour. Luckily he offered me a lift, because he works near here.

[Pause]

The first picture is correct so there is a tick in box A.

Look at the three pictures for Question 1 now.

[Pause]

Now we are ready to start. Listen carefully. You will hear each recording twice.

One. What regular exercise does David do at the moment?

Cathy: You're looking well, David! Have you been to the gym a lot recently or something?

David: Well, I joined a gym earlier this year, but I stopped going – it was just too difficult. And expensive, too! I've done a lot of swimming instead, and I feel much better for it!

Cathy: It shows! I'm thinking of taking up tennis again. Would you be interested in a game one day? You used to be quite good, didn't you?

David: Well, I haven't played for a long time but . . . why not?

[Pause]

Now listen again.

[The recording is repeated]

[Pause]

Two. What should Suzie take to Emma's house?

Woman: Suzie? It's Emma. We've got to make some paper flowers so the classroom looks nice for the end-of-term party. Can you come to my house this evening to help me do it? There's some paint left over from last time, but I can't find any brushes. Have you got one? Bring it if you have. And if we have a pair of scissors each, we can work faster, so don't forget yours. We'll need coloured paper, but I'm getting that from college. See you around six.

[Pause]

Now listen again.

[The recording is repeated]

[Pause]

Three. Which kind of T-shirt did the boy choose?

Girl: Look, it's your present. Just choose a T-shirt and then you can have anything you like printed on it. They've got three types – a picture like this one with boats on, or there are some with words, and this type has shapes on it.

Boy: Well, I really don't like writing – it makes me feel like an advertisement! And those pictures are awful . . .

Girl: Right then, I know which one you'll choose . . .

[Pause]

Now listen again.

[The recording is repeated]

[Pause]

Four. What frightened the man?

Woman: How was your camping holiday in Africa?

Man: Oh . . . fantastic . . . we saw all sorts of wildlife. You know, lots of lions and all that.

Woman: Wasn't it frightening with all those animals so close to your tent?

Man: Not really, to be honest, what scared me most were the bats . . . they flew so close at night . . . I thought I'd be frightened of all the other things like elephants . . . but in the end I wasn't because we only saw them during the day and they were mostly quite a long way away.

[Pause]

Now listen again.

[The recording is repeated]

[Pause]

Five. Where is the man calling from?

Man: Hello, Mary. Could you come and collect me? I went to a client's house by taxi, and I can't get one back.

Woman: Sure, where are you exactly?

Man: You know the bridge over the river on the North Road? If you go over that and take the first left, you see a bar on the right. I'll be waiting there. I'm actually in the farmhouse down the road from there at the moment – Mrs Collins has been kind enough to let me use her phone.

Woman: Fine, see you in the bar soon.

[Pause]

Now listen again.

[The recording is repeated]

[Pause]

Six. How did the woman spend her last holiday?

Man: You're looking well. How was your holiday in the mountains?

Woman: Not so good. I hurt my foot on the day I arrived, so climbing was just impossible. While everyone else was going off to the mountains, I stayed and read a book by the hotel pool . . . not my idea of a good holiday . . .

Man: Sorry to hear that. Well, at least you had a good rest . . . Is your foot better now?

Woman: Not really. I sit and watch television a lot and try to be patient.

[Pause]

Now listen again.

[The recording is repeated]

[Pause]

Seven. Where is the girl's purse?

Girl: Mum, I'm just off to the shop. Oh, wait a minute, where's my money?

Woman: Oh, I found your purse lying on the table earlier, so I put it back in your bag.

Key

Girl: Well, it's not in there now. Maybe it's fallen on the floor somewhere. Can you help me look under the sofa? That's where I was sitting a minute ago.

Woman: Just a minute, let *me* check. Yes, look, it *is* in here after all. I told you that's where I'd put it. You just didn't look properly!

[Pause]

Now listen again.

[The recording is repeated]

[Pause]

That is the end of Part 1.

[Pause]

Now turn to Part 2, questions 8–13.

PART 2   *You will hear a radio interview with a ballet dancer called Elena Karpov, who is talking about her life and career.*

For each question, put a tick in the correct box. You now have forty-five seconds to look at the questions for Part 2.

[Pause]

Now we are ready to start. Listen carefully. You will hear the recording twice.

Interviewer: My guest today is the star of the London Ballet Company, twenty-two-year-old Elena Karpov. Elena, you were born in Bulgaria. Did you always want to be a dancer?

Elena: Well, I was a very lively little girl, so at the age of seven my mother sent me to gymnastics classes. When I was nine, I went on to ballet lessons and from that moment I knew that I wanted to spend my life dancing. Two years later, when I was eleven, I won a place at the New York Ballet School.

Interviewer: So you had to move to the United States. Did you miss your family?

Elena: Oh yes. At first it was difficult being away from home and not knowing a lot of English. But it taught me how to look after myself and not to depend on others. There were other Bulgarian students there, and we actually found it quite easy to learn enough English to take part in the lessons with the other students.

Interviewer: Tell us about your latest role with the London Ballet Company.

Elena: I'm going to dance the part of *Cinderella*. It's a story about a poor girl who marries a handsome prince. My parents used to read it to me when I was little. I'd never seen the ballet before, but I already knew the music really well. I'm sure children will love the ballet.

Interviewer: What do you do when you're not practising or performing?

Elena: Before I joined this company I spent two weeks going round London as a tourist. I don't have time for sightseeing now, but I love trying on the latest fashions with my friends. I'm always buying new jeans and trainers! I'm not too keen on discos and nightclubs – I dance enough during the day!

Interviewer: You must have lots of fans.

Elena: Quite a few! They always ask for a photograph of me, but unfortunately I don't have many to give away. I sometimes sign their programmes instead, and if I can I give them one of the flowers I've received from the audience. They always ask for tickets, but of course that's not possible.

Interviewer: What's been the best thing that's happened in your career so far?

Elena: Well, I've been a guest dancer with ballet companies in Moscow and Vienna, and I appeared twice on television in Bulgaria and met the president! I shall never forget that! But the most satisfying thing for me is that I'm paid for doing what I really enjoy – dancing!

Interviewer: Elena, thank you for talking to us.

Elena: Thank you.

[Pause]

Now listen again.

[The recording is repeated]

[Pause]

That is the end of Part 2.

[Pause]

Now turn to Part 3, questions 14–19.

PART 3   *You will hear a group leader talking to some students who are going to visit an important athletics event in Birmingham.*

For each question, fill in the missing information in the numbered space. You now have twenty seconds to look at Part 3.

[Pause]

Now we are ready to start. Listen carefully. You will hear the recording twice.

Teacher: Right everyone! Some important information about the three college trips before the end of June. Firstly, we're all going to Birmingham to see the International Athletics Championships. That's the only trip we've planned during March because I know that April is such a busy time for students. We're going on the 15th. For those of you who haven't heard of this event before, it's the largest single sports competition in Britain, so we're really pleased that we're going. A hundred and forty different national teams will take part, which means you'll see five hundred and twenty world-class sportsmen and women there, and you'll be amongst thousands of other fans. The stadium seats seventeen thousand!

We'll be leaving here early and we've decided to go by train this time and not hire a coach, because we got delayed in traffic jams when we went to Birmingham before. I hope everyone's pleased about that.

Next, someone asked me what to take. Firstly, what *not* to take! Leave your cameras behind because taking photos is forbidden, but you *must* have your identity card with you as we've bought a group ticket, and you may need to show it. Mobile phones are okay, but you'll have to turn them off during the event, so it's probably better not to take them.

If you want to read some more about the event on the Internet, go to Birmingham's website. Then look for the word 'Birinfo' in the page index, that's spelt B-I-R-I-N-F-O. You'll find all kinds of information about the Championships there.

As for our trip, I don't have the final details of journey times yet, but I will by this afternoon. So, I think I'll write an information sheet with answers to all your questions on it. You'll get copies of this on Friday, so you can read through everything over the weekend.

Right . . . the second trip will . . .

[Pause]

Now listen again.

[The recording is repeated]

[Pause]

That is the end of Part 3.

[Pause]

Now turn to Part 4, questions 20–25.

Look at the six sentences for this part.

PART 4   *You will hear two friends, a boy, Rolf, and a girl, Maria, talking about the jobs they would like to do in the future.*

Decide if each sentence is correct or incorrect. If it is correct, put a tick in the box under A for YES. If it is not correct, put a tick in the box under B for NO. You now have twenty seconds to look at the questions for Part 4.

[Pause]

Now we are ready to start. Listen carefully. You will hear the recording twice.

Maria: What do you want to do when you leave college, Rolf?

Rolf: I haven't decided yet, Maria. I might go travelling for six months, and then look for a job. How about you?

Maria: I hope to start work straight away.

Rolf: Do you know where?

Maria: Well, I'd prefer to live near my family, but I want to see the world too. So I'd hope to have plenty of trips for work.

Rolf: You could get a job with an airline company.

Maria: Mmm . . . that'd be great, but it's hard to get into.

Rolf: I know lots of people apply for that kind of work. But you're good at languages – I'm sure they'd accept you.

Maria: I hope so. Have you really not decided what job you'd like?

Rolf: It's difficult. My degree's in music, but I definitely don't want to be a music teacher. I'll probably look for something completely different.

Maria: Oh . . . that's a shame. Why not become a music teacher? You'd get long holidays.

Rolf: But if I got a job in business, I could earn far more money.

Maria: Lots of people say money doesn't matter, and you should just find a job you enjoy. But I think a job has to pay well, so you can live comfortably . . .

Rolf: Mmm . . . That's exactly how I see it.

Maria: Do you think you'll have lots of different jobs before you find a really good one?

Rolf: I expect so. No one finds the perfect job immediately . . .

Maria: I'd like to find a job I really like, and stay with the same company for at least ten years . . .

Rolf: Oh, I see, that's interesting.

Maria: Your father has his own business, doesn't he?

Rolf: Yes, but I don't want to work for him.

Maria: But he could help you set up your own business.

Rolf: I couldn't imagine doing that. I know how many hours my father has to work.

Maria: Mmm . . . your free time's important to you, isn't it?

Rolf: It certainly is!

Maria: Right . . .

[Pause]

Now listen again.

[The recording is repeated]

[Pause]

That is the end of Part 4.

[Pause]

You now have six minutes to check and copy your answers on to the answer sheet.

Note: Teacher, stop the recording here and time six minutes. Remind students when there is **one** minute remaining.

That is the end of the test.

Test 4

PAPER 1   READING AND WRITING

READING

Part 1

1 C   2 B   3 C   4 A   5 B

Part 2

6 E   7 C   8 F   9 H   10 B

Part 3

11 B   12 A   13 A   14 A   15 A   16 B   17 B   18 B   19 A
20 B

Part 4

21 B   22 A   23 C   24 D   25 A

Part 5

26 C   27 B   28 C   29 B   30 B   31 A   32 B   33 C   34 A
35 D

WRITING

Part 1

1 far (away) from
2 pay
3 took/showed the class
4 when/before
5 bored

Part 2

Task-specific Mark Scheme

The content elements that need to be covered are:

i   apology for not being able to go to the cinema
ii reason why candidate cannot go
iii details of an alternative invitation

The following sample answers can be used as a guide when marking.

SAMPLE A (Test 4, Question 6: Email to Alex)

Hello Alexd Thanks you to invited me tomorrow, but I can't went to the cinema because I was played tennis with a friend and I can't went with you. Would you went to saw my tennis match at 9:00 a.m.

Examiner Comments

The message is obscured by errors and points 1 and 3 are missing.

Mark: 2

SAMPLE B (Test 4, Question 6: Email to Alex)

Hi Alex!

I'm writing you to apologise me because toomorrow I can't go with you to the cinema. I forgot to told you that I would played a football match.

Why don't we go to the cinema after tomorrow?

See you soon

Diya

Examiner Comments

Despite the mixed use of tenses, this script sufficiently covers all points.

Mark: 4

SAMPLE C (Test 4, Question 6: Email to Alex)

Dear Alex

I'm sorry I can't go to the cinema tomorrow, because I have to visit my uncle who is ill in hospital.

How about going to the cinema the day after tomorrow?

Please a.s.a.p.

From Yoko

Examiner Comments

This is concise and accurate and above the level expected.

Mark: 5

SAMPLE D (Test 4, Question 7: Letter to a friend)

Dear Christine

I received your letter this morning. Someone else already told me that the restaurant you went to is a very nice place. I really like going out with friends and have dinner but not that often. I only go twice in a week never more than twice. Once of my favourite restaurants is "Revolution" it is a great place to meet new people and their food is delicious. If you come to my house one time I will take you out for dinner, you must have been to this restaurant it is such a nice place. Don't forget to bring your finest dress because you need be dressed smart to get in.

Examiner Comments

This is a very good effort. The language is confident and ambitious with a wide range, e.g. 'Someone else already told me . . .'. It is well organized with only a few minor errors, e.g. 'you need be dressed . . .'. It requires no effort from the reader. Note: There is no closing formula but this makes no difference to the mark.

Band: 5

SAMPLE E (Test 4, Question 7: Letter to a friend)

> *Dear Bob*
> *How are you? I often eat out once a week. I like Chinese food, so I usually go to Chinese*
> *restaurant with my friends. We usually order some meats vegertables and rice. I like try*
> *different Chinese restaurant in Lincoln but, my favourite restaurant called New Suan. I think*
> *this restaurant not very big but, there are cooking is very good. I like there meals very*
> *delicous. When you have a meal, there are play some Chinese music. I really enjoy have a meal*
> *in the restaurant. If you have a time I hope you can come to Lincoln try the restaurant.*
> *Best wishes*
> *From Jamie*

Examiner Comments

This is an inadequate attempt. The language is limited. There is some repetition, e.g. 'usually', 'There are play some Chinese music' coupled with inconsistent punctuation. There are numerous errors which show a lack of control, e.g. 'I think this restaurant . . . cooking is very good'. Considerable effort is required from the reader.

Band: 2

SAMPLE F (Test 4, Question 7: Letter to a friend)

> *Dear Ali,*
> *How are you? I am fine. Thank you! I received your letter yesterday. I was very*
> *pleased to know that you are fine.*
> *You asked me that how often I go out for eating. I usually go on weekends, with my*
> *friends. I often have candle light dinner with my girlfriend.*
> *One of my favourite resurants are Savoy, which is in central London. It is a bit*
> *expensive but I manage to afford it. I like this restaurants because I am very found*
> *of luxrious stuff, and want myself to be treated like a V.V.I.P. So, this all is done*
> *by Savoy. That's why I like going there.*
> *Yours Sincerely*
> *Syed Arslar Haider*

Examiner Comments

This is a good attempt. The language is fairly ambitious, e.g. 'I manage to afford it', 'want myself . . . V.V.I.P.'. There is a more than adequate range of structures and vocabulary. It is well organized with clear paragraphing. There are some non-impeding errors, e.g. 'I am very found of luxrious stuff' but only a little effort is required from the reader.

Band: 4

SAMPLE G **(Test 4, Question 8: Surprise story)**

> I had a real surprise when I turned on the television. I was there sitting in a park. I didn't know that place so my next task was to look at the person again. She was a girl like me with the same face, hair and everything except for her cloths. She was very untidy. Then I called the TV company where it was taken and about the details. After lots of wringling I found her. When we saw each other, we couldn't move. I asked a lot of questions about her life, parents, friends. Finally, both of us knew: SHE IS MY SISTER!!!! Now she lives with me and our parents who didn't know anything about having an other child! Something had to be wrong in the hospital 21 years ago. What a luck I turned on the TV!

Examiner Comments

This is a good attempt. The language is fairly ambitious, e.g. 'When we saw each other, we couldn't move.' Vocabulary and structures are more than adequate. The story unfolds in an organised way with evidence of linking, e.g. 'Now she lives . . . an other child'. There are some errors but they are generally non-impeding, e.g. 'After lots of wringling . . .'. Only a little effort required from the reader.

Band: 4

SAMPLE H (Test 4, Question 8: Surprise story)

> My surprise Story
> I had a real surprise when I turned on the television. It was Saturday evening at 9.30 pm. The television was showed lots of football player. Because I'm really love football that why I was so surprise. It was showed my famous players. They were all line up on the TV. Then they did a lot of skills.

Examiner Comments

This attempt is inadequate. The level of language is limited, e.g. 'I'm really love football'. Some range is in evidence but it is negated by numerous errors in PET level structures, e.g. 'It was showed my famous players', 'I'm really love football'. At 51 words including the title this is short but the mark is not affected as the language is only Band 2 anyway.

Band: 2

SAMPLE I (Test 4, Question 8: Surprise story)

> I had a real surprise when I turn on the television. I have never imagined that I would appeare on the TV one day. Since last month, Jame Oliver – the best cooker of England went to my school to do his documentary – When I was eating in the school restaurant, he came and ask me: "Have you had nice meal?". I answered him. "Well, this meal seem to be better than usual!". He sat beside me we have chat for little while. At the end he asked me that do you want to appear on the television and I answered him immidiately without doubt: "Oh, of course! That is dream of everyone." Now I am quite happy because my dream have become true.

Examiner Comments

This attempt is adequate. Language is ambitious but flawed (see below). There is an adequate range of vocabulary, with a variety of structures, e.g. 'When I was eating . . . meal'. It is fairly coherent with some linking. There are a number of errors, but mostly non-impeding, e.g. 'At the end he asked me that do you want to appear on the television'. Some, but not much, effort required from the reader.

Band: 3

PAPER 2   LISTENING

Part 1

1 A   2 A   3 C   4 B   5 A   6 A   7 A

Part 2

8 B   9 A   10 A   11 C   12 C   13 B

Part 3

14   C/cycling
15   (a) C/castles (s)
16   (in the) S/spring (time)
17   (£) 55
18   M/music
19   B/bird(s) watching

Part 4

20 B   21 B   22 A   23 B   24 A   25 A

Test 4 transcript

This is the Cambridge Preliminary English Test, Test 4.

There are four parts to the test. You will hear each part twice. For each part of the test there will be time for you to look through the questions and time for you to check your answers.

Write your answers on the question paper. You will have six minutes at the end of the test to copy your answers onto the answer sheet.

The recording will now be stopped.

Please ask any questions now, because you must not speak during the test.

[Pause]

Now open your question paper and look at Part 1.

PART 1   *There are seven questions in this part. For each question there are three pictures and a short recording. Choose the correct picture and put a tick in the box below it.*

Before we start, here is an example.

How did the woman get to work?

Woman: Oh, I'm so sorry I'm late – I missed the bus. I was trying to decide whether to walk or go back and get my bike when I saw my neighbour. Luckily he offered me a lift, because he works near here.

[Pause]

The first picture is correct so there is a tick in box A.

Look at the three pictures for Question 1 now.

[Pause]

Now we are ready to start. Listen carefully. You will hear each recording twice.

One. What did the thieves steal?

Woman: What exactly is missing, sir?

Man: I thought the thieves had taken the television set, because it wasn't in its usual place in the dining room. Then I went to check my CD player and CDs – I keep them on an antique chest of drawers. All the CDs were on the floor with the CD player. But the chest had completely disappeared. It wasn't in the garden either, which is where I found the television.

Woman: Right sir. Well, can you give me a detailed description of it?

[Pause]

Now listen again.

[The recording is repeated]

[Pause]

Two. What present will they take?

Woman: We ought to take a present if we're staying for the weekend.

Man: Let's get something a bit different. People always take flowers and it's rather hot for chocolates. What about something for the children, like a DVD? Or . . . some unbreakable glasses they can all use outside or on picnics?

Woman: Good idea. And let's get a jug to go with them. The children have probably got lots of DVDs.

[Pause]

Now listen again.

[The recording is repeated]

[Pause]

Three. What will the woman eat tonight?

Man: Hotel York.

Woman: Hello, I'm staying in your hotel tonight, and I'm arriving quite late, about ten thirty. Will there be any food available in the hotel?

Man: I'm afraid the restaurant closes at ten o'clock, but the bar does burgers and chips until midnight. And there's always the pizza place opposite which stays open late. Or we can bring sandwiches to your room if you prefer.

Woman: Fine. I won't want to eat burgers or pizza at that time of night.

[Pause]

Now listen again.

[The recording is repeated]

[Pause]

Four. How much will the girl's ticket cost?

Woman: I'm travelling from Banbury to Witney tomorrow, and I need to be there about ten in the morning. Can you tell me when the trains leave, and how much a single ticket is?

Man: The eight thirty-five train gets in at nine forty. That's twelve pounds sixty-five for a single. The train after that leaves at nine ten and arrives at ten fifteen. That costs less because you're travelling after nine. The fare is ten pounds forty-five.

Woman: I'll take the second train. Just after ten is fine. Thanks.

[Pause]

Now listen again.

[The recording is repeated]

[Pause]

Five. What is the grandmother's job now?

Woman: My grandmother always wanted to be a teacher when she was a little girl, but she had to leave school when she was fourteen and help *her* mother clean offices and shops. When she was in her thirties she went to college, but she had to work as a waitress in the evenings to pay for her studies. A few years later she finally got the job she'd always wanted and she's done it ever since.

[Pause]

Now listen again.

[The recording is repeated]

[Pause]

Six. Which button has the boy lost?

Boy: I've lost a button on my favourite shirt. I could see that it was loose when I put it on last night. If it was the one on my pocket you wouldn't notice, but on the collar it's different. It's easy to see that it's missing from there.

Woman: Why don't you take one off your sleeve and use that. Here, you'll need some scissors. Be careful you don't cut the material.

Boy: Okay, will you sew it on for me?

Woman: Do it yourself! It's easy.

Key

[Pause]

Now listen again.

[The recording is repeated]

[Pause]

Seven. What will the man do first?

Man: Before we start painting I'll wash the kitchen floor because it's really dirty.

Woman: It'll be easier if you sweep it before you do that, Nick. I'll carry on cleaning the windows.

Man: OK, and then we can start painting the walls.

[Pause]

Now listen again.

[The recording is repeated]

[Pause]

That is the end of Part 1.

[Pause]

Now turn to Part 2, questions 8–13.

PART 2   *You will hear Sarah Brown talking about her work as a television weather forecaster. For each question, put a tick in the correct box. You now have forty-five seconds to look at the questions for Part 2.*

[Pause]

Now we are ready to start. Listen carefully. You will hear the recording twice.

Woman: Hello, I'm Sarah Brown, and I'm here to tell you about my job as a weather forecaster. I've been a weather forecaster for a television company for seven years, and two years ago I became the head of the weather department. Now, I divide my time equally between presenting weather forecasting on television and managing the weather department which has a staff of eleven. At thirty years old I'm the youngest ever head of weather and the first woman to do the job.

Since our news and weather service goes out all round the world, we all take turns to work at night. I prefer that to doing the show when I have to get up at four in the morning. I normally work an eight-hour day and in that time I do ten or twelve forecasts.

Before doing a weather forecast, I study data on the computer. This is the information I use in my forecasts. There isn't much time to learn what I have to say, but fortunately I've never forgotten my words so I don't get nervous.

My husband and I try to have the same free days, but neither of us has a regular pattern of work. He's a pilot on long-distance flights, so although he works hard he has a lot more time at home than I do. We moved to our present house about a year ago, and he's enjoying painting it.

I took up flying as a hobby five years ago. I hope to get my pilot's licence this year, but because of the job, I haven't been to the flying school for ages. For exercise I swim and ski and I like running. I'm really proud of myself for running in the London Marathon – it's a forty-kilometre race and I never thought I could manage it! My husband plays tennis, and we sometimes play together, but he's better than me so I never win.

Because I'm on world news, people sometimes recognise me in really distant places. Once, in an Indian village, an old man took me to have my photo taken with all his family. I get some lovely letters – one person wrote to say that my smile made her feel happy all day. People occasionally even write and ask me to marry them!

[Pause]

Now listen again.

[The recording is repeated]

That is the end of Part 2.

[Pause]

Now turn to Part 3, questions 14–19.

PART 3 *You will hear a radio talk about holidays in Northumberland.*

For each question, fill in the missing information in the numbered space. You now have twenty seconds to look at Part 3.

[Pause]

Now we are ready to start. Listen carefully. You will hear the recording twice.

Man: Good morning! This morning on 'Holiday Time' I want to tell you about the cycling trip I took recently to Northumberland in the north of England. Before I went I read a book by Peter Green whose title is *Cycling around Northumberland*, which I found really useful when planning my route.

Northumberland is a beautiful area of England and perfect for cycling. There is very little traffic on the roads and plenty to see and do. For example, why not visit a castle? More of them are open to the public here than in any other part of the country. While I was there I actually stayed in a flat in a castle, but there are many hotels, cottages or bed and breakfast places to choose from. In the summer it is important to book in advance, but I recommend going in the spring, as it is not so difficult to find somewhere to stay at that time of the year. You will find that some places are closed in winter.

Most of the small towns in the area have cycling centres where you can hire a bicycle. A week's hire will cost thirty-five pounds, two weeks will be fifty-five pounds. There is also a deposit of fifty pounds, which you get back when you return the bicycle.

Try to plan your holiday when there is a local event or festival happening. I went in June and was lucky enough to go to a festival of local food. Every August there's an international festival of music, but you'll find something going on in almost every month of the year.

Ring the Northumberland National Park if you're interested in finding out about their activities – they have a programme of guided walks, photography and bird watching. Ring them on double eight double 0 four six.

[Pause]

Now listen again.

[The recording is repeated]

That is the end of Part 3.

[Pause]

Now turn to Part 4, questions 20–25.

PART 4 *Look at the six sentences for this part. You will hear a conversation between a girl called Julia and her father, about choosing a course at university.*

Decide if each sentence is correct or incorrect. If it is correct, put a tick in the box under A for YES. If it is not correct, put a tick in the box under B for NO. You now have twenty seconds to look at the questions for Part 4.

[Pause]

Key

Now we are ready to start. Listen carefully. You will hear the recording twice.

Dad: So you'd better decide which university course you're going to do, Julia. You really can't delay this much longer.

Julia: But I'm in no hurry, Dad. It's ages before I *have* to decide. The main problem is that I know I'd really love to do business studies, but a lot of my friends say it sounds so boring, especially my friend Anna.

Dad: What's she going to study?

Julia: Film studies. It does look exciting in comparison.

Dad: I can see that business studies might sound dull to your friends, Julia, but you know that's far from the truth.

Julia: I know.

Dad: And don't forget that with business knowledge, you might find it much easier to get a job at the end of your degree. I'm sure your friend Anna will enjoy doing film studies, and if she's lucky, she'll get a job she enjoys. But there aren't many jobs in the film industry, so if I were her, I'd look for a different course.

Julia: You're probably right, but it *is* what Anna wants to do. Oh, I find it really difficult to decide. You don't think that business studies will be a bit too hard for me, do you?

Dad: Of course not!

Julia: And did I tell you? Jim Brooks said he'd employ me in their accounts department in the summer holidays if I chose business. I told him I really liked working with numbers and of course, I always got good marks in maths at school – not like French, which I *never* did well in.

Dad: Well, what about considering economics? That might interest you more and you might find a job working for an international bank or something.

Julia: I'd never have thought of that, Dad. No one at college has ever suggested economics. I'll go and look up some information on the Internet right away. You're such a help. Thanks.

[Pause]

Now listen again.

[The recording is repeated]

That is the end of Part 4.

[Pause]

You now have six minutes to check and copy your answers on to the answer sheet.

Note: Teacher, stop the recording here and time six minutes. Remind students when there is **one** minute remaining.

That is the end of the test.

SAMPLE

Candidate Name
If not already printed, write name
in CAPITALS and complete the
Candidate No. grid (in pencil).

Candidate Signature

Examination Title

Centre

Supervisor:
If the candidate is ABSENT or has WITHDRAWN shade here ▭

Centre No.

Candidate No.

Examination
Details

0	0	0	0
1	1	1	1
2	2	2	2
3	3	3	3
4	4	4	4
5	5	5	5
6	6	6	6
7	7	7	7
8	8	8	8
9	9	9	9

PET Paper 1 Reading and Writing Candidate Answer Sheet 1

Instructions

Use a PENCIL (B or HB).

Rub out any answer you want to change with an eraser.

For **Reading**:
Mark ONE letter for each question.
For example, if you think **A** is the right answer to the
question, mark your answer sheet like this:

0   A B C D

Part 1	Part 2	Part 3	Part 4	Part 5
1 A B C	6 A B C D E F G H	11 A B	21 A B C D	26 A B C D
2 A B C	7 A B C D E F G H	12 A B	22 A B C D	27 A B C D
3 A B C	8 A B C D E F G H	13 A B	23 A B C D	28 A B C D
4 A B C	9 A B C D E F G H	14 A B	24 A B C D	29 A B C D
5 A B C	10 A B C D E F G H	15 A B	25 A B C D	30 A B C D
		16 A B		31 A B C D
		17 A B		32 A B C D
		18 A B		33 A B C D
		19 A B		34 A B C D
		20 A B		35 A B C D

Continue on the other side of this sheet ➡

153

S A M P L E

For **Writing (Parts 1 and 2):**

Write your answers clearly in the spaces provided.

Part 1: Write your answers below.	Do not write here
1	1 1 0
2	1 2 0
3	1 3 0
4	1 4 0
5	1 5 0

Part 2 (Question 6): Write your answer below.

Put your answer to Writing Part 3 on Answer Sheet 2 ⟹

Do not write below (Examiner use only)					
0	1	2	3	4	5

S A M P L E

Candidate Name
If not already printed, write name
in CAPITALS and complete the
Candidate No. grid (in pencil).

Candidate Signature

Examination Title

Centre

Supervisor:

If the candidate is ABSENT or has WITHDRAWN shade here ▭

Centre No.

Candidate No.

Examination
Details

0	0	0	0
1	1	1	1
2	2	2	2
3	3	3	3
4	4	4	4
5	5	5	5
6	6	6	6
7	7	7	7
8	8	8	8
9	9	9	9

PET Paper 1 Reading and Writing   Candidate Answer Sheet 2

Candidate Instructions:

Write your answer to Writing Part 3
on the other side of this sheet.

→

Use a PENCIL (B or HB).

This section for use by FIRST Examiner only

Mark:

0	1.1	1.2	1.3	2.1	2.2	2.3	3.1	3.2	3.3	4.1	4.2	4.3	5.1	5.2	5.3

Examiner Number:

0	1	2	3	4	5	6	7	8	9
0	1	2	3	4	5	6	7	8	9
0	1	2	3	4	5	6	7	8	9
0	1	2	3	4	5	6	7	8	9

PET RW 2   DP492/390

S A M P L E

Do not write below this line

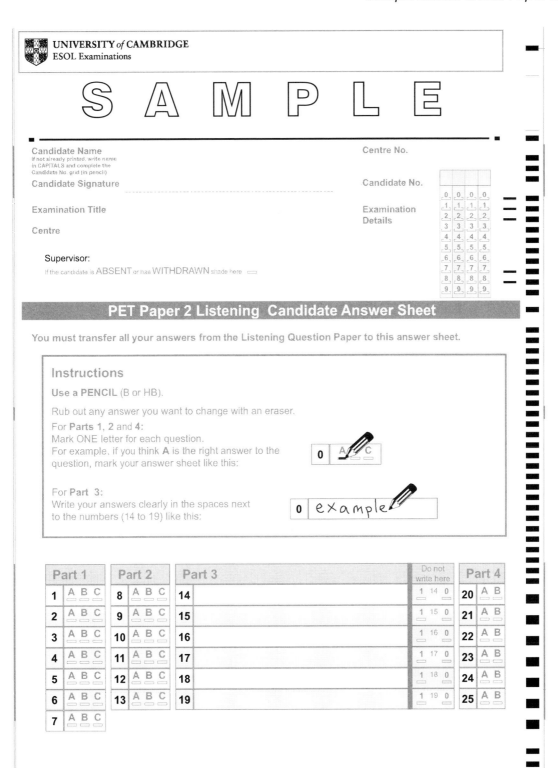

Acknowledgements

The authors and publishers acknowledge the following sources of copyright material and are grateful for the permissions granted. While every effort has been made, it has not always been possible to identify the sources of all the material used, or to trace all copyright holders. If any omissions are brought to our notice, we will be happy to include the appropriate acknowledgements on reprinting.

Royal Academy of Arts for the adapted text on p. 38 'Craigie Aitchison' by Laura Gascoigne. First published in *RA Magazine* number 80, Autumn 2003, the magazine of the Royal Academy of Arts. Reproduced by permission.

Colour section

Alamy for p. II(2C)/Simon Barber; Getty Images for p. VI(3B)/ Shuji Kobayashi; Masterfile for pp. IV(1C)/Andrew Olney, VI(4C)/David Mendelsohn, VIII(3C)/Paul Wright; Stockbroker for pp. II(1C)/Goodshoot, VIII(4B)/Martin Ley.

Black and white section

Alamy for pp. 74(10)/Blue Moon Stock; Asian Woman magazine www.asianwomanmag.com for p. 58; Corbis for p. 57/Vince Streano; Getty Images for p. 14(7) and p. 34(10)/Nisian Hughes, p. 34(6)/Jetta Productions, p. 34(7)/Harald Eisenberger, p. 54(8)/Yellow Dog Productions, p. 60/Arctic-Images, p. 74(9)/Ariel Skelley; PA Photos for p. 20/Patrick Seeger/DPA; Photofusion Picture Library for p. 74(8)/Ute Klaphake; Photolibrary.com for p. 14(6 & 8)/Monkey Business Images Ltd, p. 14(10)/Michael Turek, p. 34(9)/Stockbroker, p. 54(6)/Rudolf Reiner, p. 54(7)/Richard Ross, p. 54(9)/Jeremy Maude, p. 54(10)/Paul Thomas, p. 74(7)/ Bananastock, Punchstock for p. 34(8)/imagenavi; Shutterstock for pp. 14(9), 74(6).

Picture research by Kevin Brown.

Design concept by Peter Ducker MSTD

The CDs which accompany this book were recorded at dsound, London